Table of Contents

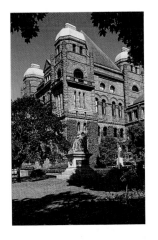

All terms appearing in boldfaced type in the text are defined in the Glossary on pages 78–80.

 anada is the second largest country in the world. It is made up of ten **provinces** and three **territories**. Bordered by three oceans—the Atlantic in the east, the Pacific in the west, and the Arctic in the north—Canada has the longest coastline of any country in the world.

*Canada is the best country in the world in which to live.
—United Nations*

CANADA IS A LAND OF SCENERY

Millions of tourists visit our amazing country each year. They come to see

- the rugged mountains of British Columbia
- the charming fishing villages and the highest tides in the world in the Atlantic provinces
- the only walled city in North America—Quebec City
- one of the wonders of the world—Niagara Falls
- the cold, striking beauty of the Arctic **tundra**
- the prairie wheat waving in the wind

The list is endless!

CANADA IS A LAND OF TREES

Almost half of Canada's land area is covered in forest, which is home to hundreds of different wild animals and birds. The products that are made from the trees in these forests are used throughout Canada and in many other countries.

CANADA IS A LAND OF WATER

Much of northern Canada is covered by thousands of lakes and rivers. Canada has the most fresh water of any country in the world.

CANADA IS A LAND OF MINERALS

Almost every important mineral known to humans can be found somewhere in Canada. Minerals are mined, or taken from the earth, and are used to make products. Even though we may not see the minerals, each day every Canadian uses something made from minerals.

In this air photo of Niagara Falls, you can see the Canadian side on the right and the American side on the left. About 170 million litres of water flow over the falls each minute.

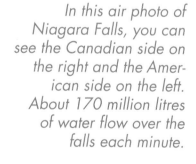

CANADA IS A LAND OF MANY PEOPLES

The **Aboriginal peoples** have lived here for thousands of years. They are the original inhabitants of the land we now call Canada. During the 1500s, the French settled on farms and in villages along the St. Lawrence River. The British were also exploring North America and eventually won control over Canada.

The Aboriginal peoples, the French, and the British were the first groups to live in this country. They are Canada's **founding peoples**.

Over the past 400 years, other peoples have come from countries throughout the world to settle in Canada. Today, we continue to welcome **immigrants** from around the world. Canada is truly a **multi-cultural** society.

WHERE ON EARTH IS CANADA?

Sasha's class is beginning to study Canada. The poster shows the earth as we would see it from hundreds of kilometres in space. The earth is sphere shaped—in other words, it is like a large ball. You can see large areas of land and a lot of water. You may recognize some of the countries.

Look at the line that runs around the middle of the earth. It is an *imaginary* line called the **equator**. The equator divides the earth exactly in half. All of the water and land above the equator are in the **northern hemisphere**. Everything below the equator is in the **southern hemisphere**. In which hemisphere is Canada?

At the top of the earth is the **North Pole**. It is always very cold and covered with ice and snow. The area around the North Pole is called the **Arctic**.

The **South Pole** is located at the bottom of the earth. It, too, is very cold and covered with ice and snow. The land around the South Pole is called the **Antarctic**.

Look at the imaginary line that starts at the North Pole and curves down to the South Pole. This is called the **prime meridian**. The prime meridian divides the earth into hemispheres as well. Everything located to the west, or left, is in the **western hemisphere**. Everything located to the east, or right, is in the **eastern hemisphere**. In which hemisphere is Canada?

In the photo, you can see that Canada is part of a large area of land that stretches from near the Arctic almost to the equator. Each large area of land in the world is called a **continent**. Canada is one of the countries located on the continent of North America.

This photo was taken by a satellite in space.

North Pole

Canada

United States

South Pole

SOMETHING TO DO

1. What country is Canada's closest neighbour?

2. Using the photo on this page as a guide, give three phrases to describe Canada's location on earth.

3. As a class, brainstorm all the good things about Canada, and list them.

still get mixed up!" said Emily. "I know north and south when I'm looking at a map. But I sometimes switch east and west."

CARDINAL DIRECTIONS

Cardinal points are the four main points of the compass: north, south, east, west.

Most maps are set up so that on the compass

- north (N) points to the top
- south (S) points to the bottom
- east (E) points to the right
- west (W) points to the left

The trick is to note that the first letters in _west_ and _east_ spell the word _we_. So you never need to mix up west and east again!

Look at the pictures on the next page. Using the compass symbol as your guide, try to answer the following questions as a class.

For example: In which direction are the ice skates from the tent? Put your finger on the picture of the tent. Then find the ice skates. In which direction does your finger move from the tent to the ice skates? If you said _west_, you gave the correct answer.

In which direction is

a) the helmet from the baseball glove?
b) the bicycle from the computer?
c) the tennis ball from the in-line skates?
d) the tree house from the football?
e) the football from the birdhouse?

INTERMEDIATE DIRECTIONS

We don't always travel straight north or south, east or west. To help us out, the compass shows in-between, or **intermediate, points**:

- northeast (NE)—between north and east
- northwest (NW)—between north and west
- southeast (SE)—between south and east
- southwest (SW)—between south and west

Look at the pictures again, and try to answer the following questions about intermediate directions. The trick here is to remember that intermediate directions always start with the words _north_ or _south_.

For example: In which direction is the birdhouse from the in-line skates? Place your finger on the picture of the in-line skates. To get to the birdhouse, are you moving your finger in a northern direction or a southern direction? Remember—always start with either the word _north_

A compass is one of the symbols usually shown on a map.

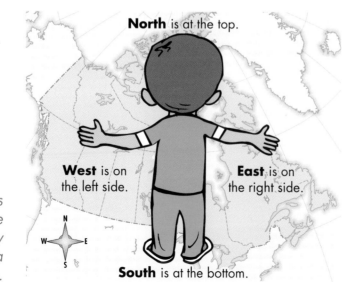

North is at the top.

West is on the left side.

East is on the right side.

South is at the bottom.

or the word *south*. Did you answer *northeast*? You are right!

In which direction is

a) the football from the helmet?
b) the tree house from the ice skates?
c) the tree house from the tennis ball?
d) the swimming pool from the baseball glove?

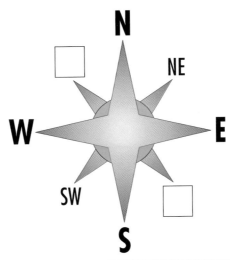

Which intermediate points should go in the empty boxes?

SOMETHING TO DO

1. Inside your classroom, determine the four cardinal directions.

2. Working in groups of four, make up directional activities for the other groups in your class.

 For example: In which direction is

 a) the teacher's desk from the door?

 b) René's desk from Marta's desk?

3. At home, figure out the following directions. In which direction are you looking when you are facing

 a) your bedroom window?   c) your kitchen window?

 b) your front doorway?   d) your living-room window?

 Ask an adult in your home to check your directions and initial them.

DID YOU KNOW?

The sun rises in the east and sets in the west wherever you are in the world.

W ow!" Emily said. "Remembering how to find west and east on the map seems easy now."

Katelyn didn't seem to be listening. She had her finger moving all over the map. Her nose was almost on the page.

"It's taking me a long time to find the places on the map," Katelyn explained. "Just searching all over the map isn't working. There must be an easier way to do this."

USING A GRID

Katelyn is right. There is an easier way to find places on a map. A **grid** is a way of using numbers and letters to find a place on a map. Below is a grid showing places that would be found in most communities. Letters and numbers are written around the edges of the grid.

The letters and numbers will help us find places on the grid. For example, the shopping mall is found at B3. Place your left finger on the letter B and your right finger on the number 3. Slide your left finger across the grid along the squares of B, and slide your right finger down the grid along the squares of 3. Did your fingers meet at the shopping mall? If they did, you are in the right place!

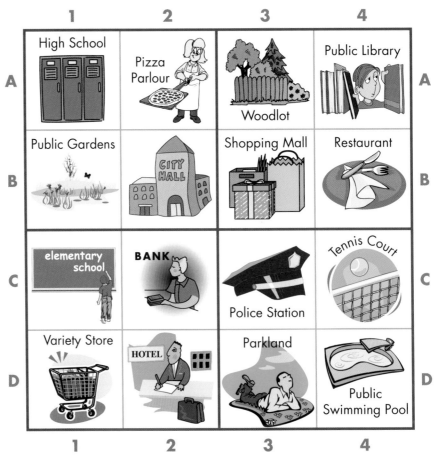

Latitude and Longitude

As a class, name the places found in the following squares:

a) C2
b) A4
c) D3
d) A1
e) B4
f) D1
g) C3
h) B1

In which squares are the following places?

a) the hotel
b) the tennis court
c) city hall
d) the woodlot
e) the elementary school
f) the public swimming pool

Do you remember your directions from Chapter 2? Look at the grid again. One dark line cuts horizontally across the centre of this community, creating a north section and a south section. The second dark line runs vertically, creating an east section and a west section.

For example, the pizza parlour is in the northwest section of the city. (Remember that the words *north* or *south* always come first.)

As a class, decide in which section of the city you would find the following:

a) the hotel
b) city hall
c) the shopping mall
d) the bank
e) the tennis court
f) the parkland
g) the public library
h) the public gardens
i) the police station

Grid lines have been drawn on the map of the Great Lakes below. Letters are shown along the side of the map, and numbers are shown across the top. These letters and numbers are called **coordinates**. What

> **DID YOU KNOW?**
>
> Lines going from side to side are called **horizontal** lines. Lines going from top to bottom are called **vertical** lines.

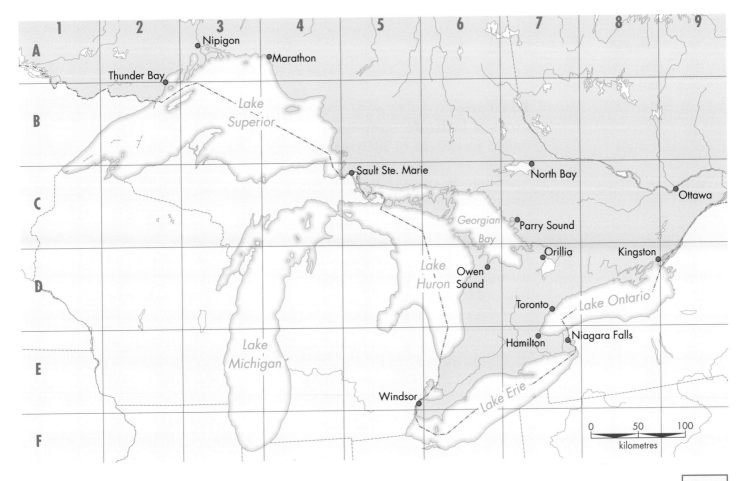

city is found at the coordinates E5?

As a class, find the following cities by using these coordinates:

a) A2
b) C5
c) D8
d) D6
e) A3

Name the coordinates of the following places:

a) Ottawa
b) Parry Sound
c) Marathon

USING LATITUDE AND LONGITUDE

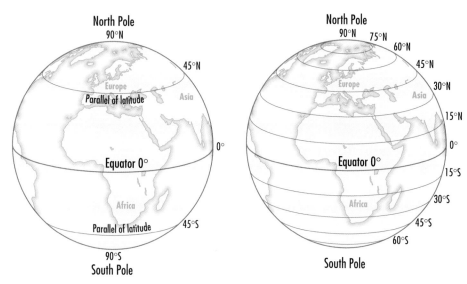

Latitude

Lines of **latitude**, sometimes called **parallels of latitude**, are imaginary lines drawn on a map. They run in the same direction around the globe as the equator. Lines of latitude help people locate places north and south of the equator. They are measured in units called *degrees*. The symbol for degree is °.

As a class, answer the following questions:

a) If you wanted to find a city located at 45 degrees north (45° N) latitude, would you look above or below the equator?

b) How many degrees north latitude is the North Pole?

c) How many degrees south latitude is the South Pole?

d) Which of the following is closest to the equator: 15° N latitude or 45° S latitude?

Longitude

Lines of **longitude**, sometimes called **meridians of longitude**, are also imaginary lines drawn on a map. These lines run north and south like the prime meridian. They help people locate places east and west of the prime meridian. They are also measured in degrees.

As a class, answer the following:

a) Which is the most important meridian of longitude to help you find places east or west on the map?

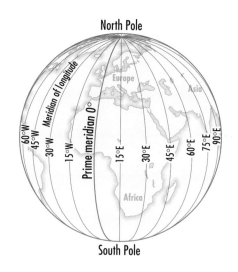

b) Which of the following is closer to the prime meridian: 30° W longitude or 15° E longitude?

When lines of latitude and lines of longitude are drawn on a map, they form a grid that looks similar to the one we saw on the map of the Great Lakes.

Look at the map of the world

Latitude and Longitude

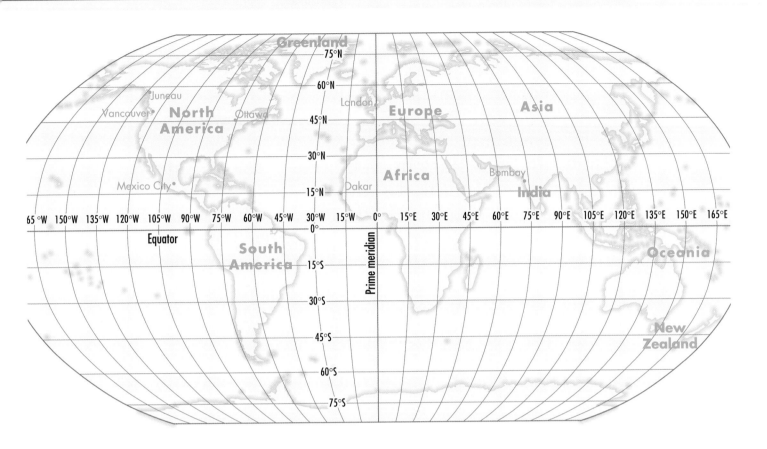

above. Notice that the lines of longitude and latitude are marked in degrees. Review the names of the continents.

Using these coordinates, find the following continents:

a) 55° N, 100° E (Hint: It will be in the northern and eastern hemispheres.)
b) 15° S, 60° W
c) 15° N, 15° E

d) 20° S, 125° E
e) 60° N, 120° W

Find the following countries:

a) 30° S, 135° E
b) 15° N, 75° E

Find the following cities:

a) 45° N, 75° W
b) 49° N, 123° W
c) 55° N, 0°

SOMETHING TO DO

1. Name two continents on the equator.

2. Name one continent that is completely in the northern and western hemispheres.

3. Through which city does the prime meridian run?

4. Working in pairs, find five places on the globe. Work out the coordinates. Exchange your coordinates with another pair of students. Name the places they found.

hose imaginary latitude and longitude lines and an atlas sure made map reading easier," confessed Katelyn.

"I ran into some *real* imaginary lines this weekend," Nathan said.

"How can imaginary lines be real?" asked Katelyn, rolling her eyes. "I think it's impossible!"

"You're right in a way," admitted Nathan, "but *I'm* right in a way, too. We visited Niagara Falls, and I stood with one foot in the United States and one foot in Canada. That part was real. So there had to be a boundary or borderline running between my feet, even though there wasn't one . . . really."

"I think I'll stick to the soccer boundary lines. At least I can see them," Katelyn said, as she ran out to the field.

United States (Alaska)

DID YOU KNOW?

An *atlas* is a book of maps.

This photograph shows a border crossing between Quebec and Vermont (USA).

BOUNDARY LINES

Boundary lines are like the lines going around the outside edge of a soccer, football, or baseball field. The games are played inside these boundary lines. **Cartographers**—people who make maps—draw boundary lines and borderlines on maps so that we can see the area of each province and country.

WHAT IS A POLITICAL MAP?

A **political map** is one where boundary lines and borderlines are shown. This type of map can also show provinces, the capitals, cities, towns, main roads, railways, and waterways.

Reading the Map

To read the map, you need to know what symbols the cartographer has used. This information is found in a **key**, or **legend**, included on the map.

What information is given to you in the key on this map? How many provinces are there in Canada? How many territories? Name the **capital city** of your province or territory.

Using the map key as a guide, as a class name each province and territory and its capital. Then divide into pairs. Without looking at the map, one partner will name as many provinces and territories—and their capitals—as possible. The other partner will check the answers by looking at the map. Now switch roles with your partner.

Vancouver
Island

Victoria

Pacific Ocean

SOMETHING TO DO

1. a) In what direction is the Yukon from

   • Ottawa?   • Alberta?   • British Columbia?

   b) In what direction is Winnipeg from

   • Newfoundland and Labrador?   • Nunavut?
   • Ontario?

2. Which provinces border on an ocean?

3. Name the lake that is

   a) 66° N, 120° W   b) 53° N, 80° W

4. On an outline map of Canada

   a) locate and label the provinces, the territories, the provincial capitals, Canada's capital, and the oceans

   b) draw the borderline between Canada and the United States in purple

   c) colour the Maritime provinces in red, the Prairie provinces in green, and the Great Lakes in blue

Canada has more fresh water than any other country in the world. Its rivers, lakes, and streams carry huge amounts of water down mountain ranges, through valleys, across the plains, and even through the frozen Arctic.

Water is constantly moving from a higher level to a lower level. Look at the drawing of the river system. Follow the river from its beginning, on higher land, to its end, where the land is lower.

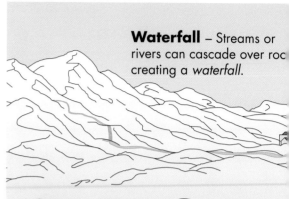

Waterfall – Streams or rivers can cascade over roc creating a *waterfall*.

Source – The *source* is where a river begins. It could be the place where spring water, rainwater, or melting ice/snow starts to run down a slope. It could also be where water flows out of a lake.

River – A *river* is a large stream of water flowing along a definite path, or channel.

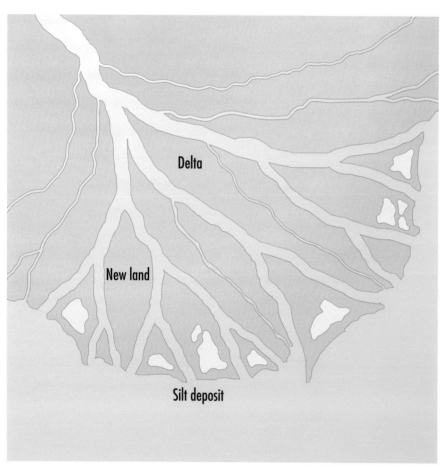

Delta

New land

Silt deposit

This is an illustration of a fan-shaped delta.

Where Do Our Rivers Go?
Most rivers in Canada drain northward to the Arctic Ocean, Hudson Bay, and Hudson Strait. The rest drain into the Pacific or Atlantic Oceans, with a small portion draining southward into the United States.

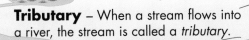

Tributary – When a stream flows into a river, the stream is called a *tributary*.

w – A river *flows* from higher
d to lower land, away from its
ce, or beginning.

Branch – When two streams of equal size meet, one is often referred to as a *branch*.

Meander – As the river reaches flatter land, it flows more slowly. It curves and bends in S-shaped loops called *meanders*.

Stream – The spring water, rainwater, or melting ice/snow collect in channels, or *streams*.

Oxbow lakes – The cuttings on the outside of a meander cause the loops to grow bigger. Some of these meanders are cut off and left behind as *oxbow lakes*.

uth – The place
ere a river flows into
rger body of water,
h as an ocean, sea,
, or marsh, is called
mouth.

Delta – Some rivers dump mud and sand as they slow down to flow into other bodies of water. The mud and sand build up areas of land. This built-up land makes a fan-shaped *delta*.

Flood plain – When a river floods, it deposits silt and other sediments across the floor of its valley. The area covered by the flood waters is called a *flood plain*.

This illustration shows the main parts of a river system.

SOMETHING TO DO

1. a) Place some gravel, sand, dried grasses, and water into a large jar. Close the lid tightly.

   b) Shake the jar well. Record what happens to the materials in the jar.

   c) Record what happens to the materials as the water movement slows down.

   d) Record the order in which the materials settle.

   e) Compare what happens to the materials in the jar to what happens when the flow of a river begins to slow down.

2. Using an atlas, find the source of the Fraser River in British Columbia. Where is the mouth of the river?

3. Using Plasticine, make a model of a river system. To see if it works, test your river system by pouring a small amount of water at the source.

DID YOU KNOW?

The Mackenzie River is the longest river in Canada.

ow did you guess so quickly that it was my silhouette?" asked Samantha.

"It's easy," said Erin. "I recognized your physical features—the shapes on your face that make you look like *you!*"

The starting point for measuring elevation (the height of land) is the level of the sea. A place may be located above, at, or below sea level.

NATURE'S PHYSICAL FEATURES

Just as Erin, Samantha, and you have physical features made by nature, the surface of the earth also has physical features such as hills, mountains, and flatlands. These features are called **landforms**.

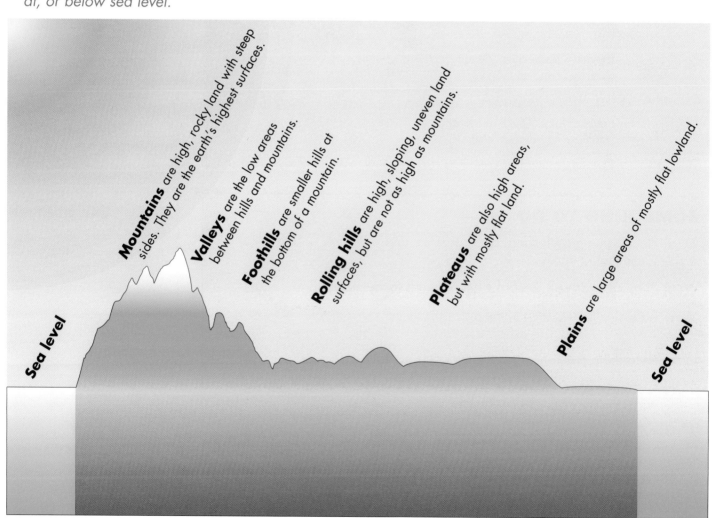

Mountains are high, rocky land with steep sides. They are the earth's highest surfaces.

Valleys are the low areas between hills and mountains.

Foothills are smaller hills at the bottom of a mountain.

Rolling hills are high, sloping, uneven land surfaces, but are not as high as mountains.

Plateaus are also high areas, but with mostly flat land.

Plains are large areas of mostly flat lowland.

Sea level

Sea level

HOW MOVING WATER CAN SHAPE THE EARTH'S FEATURES

Have you ever poured water over a sand pile and watched how the water runs off in different directions? The longer you pour the water over the sand, the more the shape of the pile changes.

Many of the earth's natural features have been shaped by the action of moving water. Heavy rain or melting ice and snow cause mountain streams and rivers to become very fast flowing. Loose soil, mud, and pieces of rock and pebbles are picked up and carried along in the flow. The sharp edges of the rocks and pebbles act as cutting tools. They are rolled, tumbled, and bounced along the sides and bottom of the **stream bed**, the land over which the river or stream flows. After thousands of years, features such as deep v-shaped valleys begin to form in the sides of a mountain.

Over thousands of years, other natural actions or forces cause the shape of the earth to change. Some of these forces include

- the blowing of the wind
- the pelting of rain and sleet
- the movement of thick, heavy ice sheets called **glaciers**
- volcanic eruptions
- earthquakes

THE PHYSICAL REGIONS OF CANADA

Nature has made it easy for us to divide Canada into seven **regions**, or large areas. Each region is identified by one main physical feature common to the region. The smaller features are then identified within the main region. Look at the map on pages 16–17.

*This illustration shows a stream valley. The stream has caused **erosion**, or the wearing away of the rock over a long period of time.*

Wind is the movement of air. High winds can erode boulders, causing them to take on different shapes.

*Winds can blow sand into huge piles called **dunes**.*

This map shows the physical regions of Canada.

The Cordillera region is found on the west coast of Canada.

Physical features:

This region is mainly a chain, or ridge, of high mountains, including the Rocky Mountains. Grasses grow on the high mountain areas, and forests on the slopes. The rock has valuable mineral deposits. There are plateaus, deep, fertile valleys, and a seacoast.

The Canadian Shield region, shaped like a horseshoe with Hudson Bay in the middle, covers more than half of Canada.

Physical features:

This huge region has mainly rounded hills of ancient rock. Much of this rock is covered with thin soil, although there are many areas of just bare rock. The soil is poor for farming, but coniferous forests thrive on it. The rock contains valuable minerals. Many thousands of lakes, fast-flowing rivers, and swamps cover the region.

Arctic Ocean

Arctic Lowland

Cordillera

Canadian Shield

Interior Plains

Pacific Ocean

Key

	Appalachian Highlands
	Great Lakes - St. Lawrence Lowlands
	Canadian Shield
	Interior Plains
	Hudson Bay Lowlands
	Cordillera
	Arctic Lowlands
⬭	Ice cap
⎓	Marshland

The Interior Plains region covers central Canada. This includes the three Prairie provinces.

Physical features:

This region is mainly hundreds of kilometres of open, flat, fertile land in the south. It is excellent for growing grains, especially wheat, and grasses for grazing. Under the soil of the plains lie oil, natural gas, and minerals. Rolling hills, with coniferous trees on the slopes, are found in the north.

Landforms and Physical Regions

The Arctic Lowlands region lies almost entirely within the Arctic Circle. It covers more than one-quarter of Canada's land surface, including a number of barren islands.

Physical features:

This region is mainly rocky and marshy. The ground is covered in ice and snow for most of the year. Lichen, mosses, and low-lying shrubs grow here.

The Hudson Bay Lowlands region is found mainly on the southern end of Hudson Bay in Northern Ontario.

Physical features:

This region is mostly a plain of low-lying flat, marshy land. Grass-like plants and low shrubs grow here. It is one of the largest areas of wetland in the world.

The Great Lakes-St. Lawrence Lowlands region stretches along the St. Lawrence River to the Great Lakes.

Physical features:

This region is mainly fertile lowland, which is good for farming and grazing. There are many lakes and rivers, along with some low rolling hills. On the slopes of these hills are mixed forests with **deciduous** and coniferous trees.

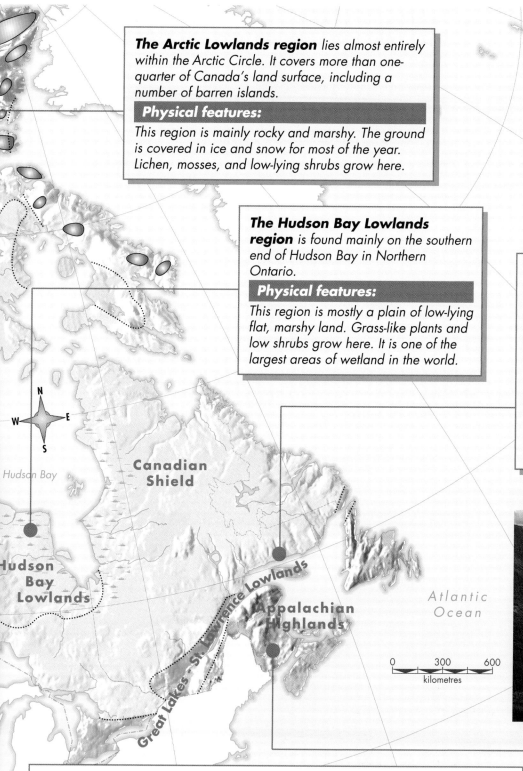

Hudson Bay

Canadian Shield

Hudson Bay Lowlands

Great Lakes - St. Lawrence Lowlands

Appalachian Highlands

Atlantic Ocean

0   300   600
kilometres

The Appalachian Highlands region is on the east coast of Canada.

Physical features:

This region is mainly an old mountain range that has been worn down by erosion. It now consists of rolling hills and broad valleys. **Coniferous** forests cover these slopes. Rich, fertile soil is found in the valleys. There are manuy rivers and lakes with spectacular steep cliffs along a long seacoast.

SOMETHING TO DO

1. Explain why fewer farms are found in the Canadian Shield region than in the Interior Plains region.

2. a) Compare the physical features of the Cordillera region to those of the Appalachian region.

   b) List the features that are common to both regions.

3. How are the Arctic Lowlands and the Hudson Bay Lowlands regions alike?

I recognize the shapes of the Great Lakes," said Ishwar. "They certainly make it easy to pick out the province of Ontario."

"I have a way to remember their names," explained Erin. "I think of the word *HOMES*—Huron, Ontario, Michigan, Erie, and Superior. Get it?"

"Got it!" replied Ishwar. "I have a way to remember their order from east to west—Only Eat Hot Meals On Sunday. Get it?"

Erin was still thinking as Ishwar left for recess.

The Great Lakes

Huron
Ontario
Michigan
Erie
Superior

THE GREAT LAKES

There are five Great Lakes. Four of them lie along the border of Canada (in Ontario) and the United States. Which lake is completely in the United States?

In Which Direction Does the Water Flow?

The water flows from Lake Superior, through all of the Great Lakes, down the St. Lawrence River, and empties into the Atlantic Ocean. **Groundwater**, lakes, rivers, tributaries, and streams are always emptying into each of the Great Lakes and the St. Lawrence River, keeping them supplied with water. If you were travelling from Lake Ontario to Lake Erie, would you be travelling *with* the flow or *against* the flow of the water?

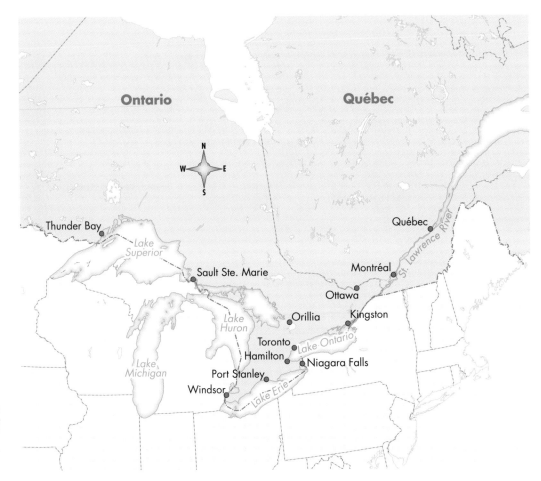

This map shows the St. Lawrence Seaway and Great Lakes Waterway.

Fresh Water

The Great Lakes are by far the largest continuous (without a break) body of fresh water on earth. This water is used by households for drinking and cooking and by factories in the manufacturing of products. What are some other household uses for water?

Recreation

Thousands of people, especially from the nearby areas, visit beaches, resorts, and provincial parks along the Great Lakes. Name some recreational activities.

Transportation

The Aboriginal peoples were the first to travel on the Great Lakes. They portaged (carried their canoes and supplies) around rapids and between lakes where the water levels changed, for example, at Niagara Falls.

The early Europeans in Canada began building water paths, or channels, to direct water around the rapids and between the Great Lakes. By 1932, many large channels, or **canals**, had been built, but most were narrow and shallow. Only smaller ships could sail through them.

In 1954, Canada and the United States decided to work together to build a seaway. The seaway was to have a number of **locks** and canals. This would make a wide, deep passageway from the Atlantic Ocean all the way inland to Lake Superior. In 1959, the St. Lawrence Seaway was completed.

THE IMPORTANCE OF THE SEAWAY

Each year, millions of tonnes of cargo such as timber, grain, oil, and minerals are carried through the seaway on large ships called freighters and tankers. These materials are delivered to **industries** (factories) located along the shores of the Great Lakes. Iron ore, for example, is shipped to Hamilton's steel mills from Quebec and Labrador. Then new cargo is loaded onto the empty freighters. This cargo is delivered to other ports along the seaway, or it is shipped down the seaway to the Atlantic Ocean to be delivered to other countries.

DID YOU KNOW?

A lockmaster is the person who opens and closes the gates of a lock.

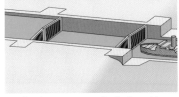

1. The ship arrives at the lock and has to go up to the next level.

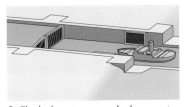

2. The lockmaster opens the lower gates of the lock. The ship enters, and the gates are closed.

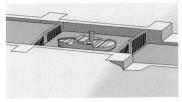

3. The lockmaster opens the valves at the upper gates. Water on the other side of the upper gates flows into the lock. The ship floats up on the rising water.

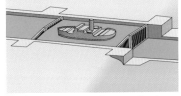

4. The water rises to the same level as the water on the other side of the upper gates.

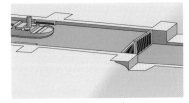

5. The lockmaster opens the upper gates, and the ship continues on its journey.

Ships use locks when there is a difference in levels between one body of water and the next. The ships are moved from one level to another by raising and lowering the water in the locks.

SOMETHING TO DO

1. Describe how a ship goes through locks from a higher water level to a lower water level.

2. Write the words *Great Lakes* vertically on a page. Each of the letters will be the first letter in a key word that is connected to the Great Lakes. You may use the first two examples below, or think of other key words.

   G is for the grain carried to other ports by freighters.

   R is for the rivers that empty into the Great Lakes.

   E is for ... (and so on).

Natural resources are materials found in nature that are useful in our daily lives. They include water, minerals, soil, animals, trees, and other vegetation. They also include fuels that we use for **energy**, such as oil and natural gas. Canada has plenty of natural resources. As a class, discuss how we might find each of these resources useful.

WHAT IS ENERGY?

We know that our bodies need food to give us energy for playing soccer, skipping rope, walking, talking, and studying. Many things that we use each day also require energy. Automobiles and lawn mowers need gas to work. Furnaces need oil or natural gas. Computers, TVs, ovens, and toasters need **electricity**. It's easy to see why oil and natural gas are called energy fuels. Electricity also provides us with energy, but where does it come from?

Suppose we had a generator as big as Erin's house. In fact, we do. Across Canada, we have many huge generators that produce electricity. But what makes these generators turn? As we'll see, many things do.

Generator

*Erin is visiting the Ontario Science Centre in Toronto. The pedals of the bicycle are attached to a small **generator** that produces electricity.*

Water Power

Water power produces much of the electricity in Canada. Falling water provides the power.

A wall is built on a river to store the water for the generator. This structure is called a dam. As water rushes down the water pipe, or the penstock, it meets the **turbine**, which is attached to the generator. (A turbine is like a modern water wheel.) The rushing water turns the turbine and generator to produce electricity. The electricity is then moved by huge power lines to cities and towns and eventually to your home to run your TV, toaster, light bulbs, and so on.

Electricity is also made in other ways. Nuclear material, oil, natural gas, or coal are burned to turn water into steam. The steam turns the turbine, which turns the generator to produce electrical energy.

Electricity is an important source of energy in Canada. We use electricity in our homes, schools, and businesses. Factories depend on it to run their machinery. Electricity lights our streets at night.

MINERALS

Almost every important mineral known can be found somewhere in Canada. Each day, every Canadian uses something made from minerals. Let's take a look.

Natural Resources: Nature's Gift

Our Homes

If all the materials made from minerals were taken from our homes, we would probably be sleeping under the stars!

- The concrete in basements contains limestone, sand, and gravel.
- The bricks on the outside of homes and the tiles in bathrooms contain clay.
- The glass in windows contains silica.
- Copper wires carry electricity throughout homes, and copper pipes deliver water to taps.
- Walls are made of gypsum.
- Even the saws, chisels, and hammers used in the building of homes are made from iron ore.

Our Lives

Life without minerals would be hard to imagine.

- Televisions and computer monitors are made of many minerals and metals, too many to list.
- Your favourite singer or rock band comes to you on compact discs. Aluminum is used to produce these CDs.
- Cars, buses, trains, and airplanes use steel and aluminum in their construction. Cobalt is used in the making of jet engines. Zinc, copper, and iron are just some of the many minerals that are needed to build cars.
- Silver is used in the film for cameras.
- Sunscreen and ointments for skin rashes contain zinc.

It's easy to see why natural resources are important to Canadians. But resources do not last forever. Will there still be enough for your children and grandchildren? We must use our resources wisely—with the future in mind.

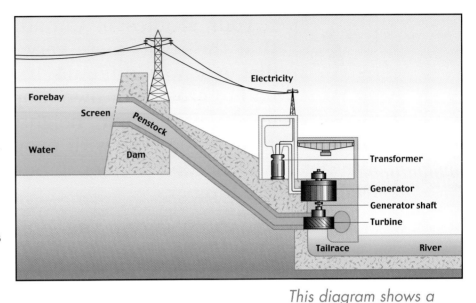

This diagram shows a hydroelectric dam and generating station.

Labels: Forebay, Screen, Water, Dam, Penstock, Electricity, Transformer, Generator, Generator shaft, Turbine, Tailrace, River

DID YOU KNOW?

Hydroelectricity is produced from the power of falling water. Thermal electricity is produced from the power of steam (by burning coal, oil, or natural gas). Nuclear plants also produce electricity by using steam power.

SOMETHING TO DO

1. Survey your class to find out how each student's home is heated (gas, oil, coal, wood, electricity, and so on). Make a bar graph to show your results.

2. a) In groups of four, brainstorm a list of items in your home and school that require electricity.

   b) Join with another group. Share and compare your lists. Together, make a general statement about the importance of electricity in our lives.

3. Using the Internet or reference books in the library, find out more about how we make use of minerals in our lives.

*I*n your studies of Canadian pioneers, you learned that the roads were very poor. Travelling any great distance was difficult. In order to survive, families had to grow their own crops. They would often **trade** goods with their neighbours. Families who had chickens might trade eggs with people who had flour. Perhaps another family needed lumber to build a new barn. They might trade flour for lumber.

TRADING AMONG THE PIONEERS

Look at the drawing below. Notice arrows A to F. What might the families have traded with each other?

The Rahm family ran a sawmill. They brought logs to their mill to make into lumber for their neighbours.

The Wilsons were wheat farmers. They also grew hay.

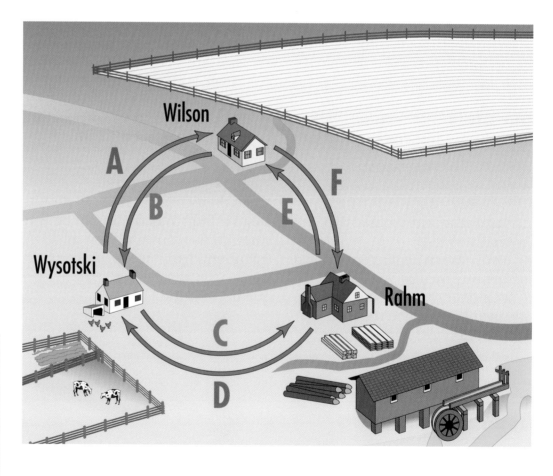

Haydon and Spencer are trading sports cards. Both boys want to trade something they have for something they want.

The Wysotski family ran a farm. They specialized in raising chickens and dairy cattle. Their farm produced a lot of eggs, milk, and butter. They had a small garden to grow vegetables for themselves.

They took the wheat to the mill to be ground into flour for making bread.

Gradually, as roads improved and became easier to travel, farmers would trade with people in the next village. Some farmers might specialize and grow only one crop such as wheat. Other farmers might specialize in raising dairy cattle. They would trade crops for goods they did not have. Some farmers would sell their farm goods for cash. With this cash, they might buy a new plough or a water pump made by the local blacksmith.

TRADING TODAY

Today, very few people trade goods as the early pioneers did. Instead, most people work for money, which they use to buy goods made anywhere in Canada or in other countries. It is more convenient. The word *trading* now refers to all the goods that are exchanged between different places in Canada, or between Canada and other countries. Millions and millions of manufactured goods, farm products, and minerals are shipped across Canada from one province to another, and to many other countries.

Look at the map of Canada on pages 10–11. Find the province of Newfoundland. It is a rocky island surrounded by ocean. The rocks make farming difficult, but the ocean is rich with seafood such as lobster and crab.

Using the same map, find a province that you think will have the fewest seafood products. You may have chosen Saskatchewan or Alberta because they do not have a shoreline on one of the three oceans of Canada. These two provinces have flat, fertile land. They grow farm products such as wheat and other grains.

Southern Ontario is the manufacturing centre of Canada. Hundreds of large and small factories produce everything from automobiles to stoves to kitchen sinks.

Discuss as a class what item each province above might trade with the other three.

Throughout this book, as we study Canada, we'll find that the physical features of each province and territory often determine what people do to earn a living. In turn, this determines what goods they produce.

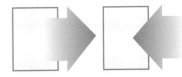

In Chapters 12 to 22, you will see arrows like these. The arrow on the left tells you what goods are sent to other provinces or **exported** to other countries. The arrow on the right tells you what goods are received from other provinces or **imported** from other countries.

SOMETHING TO DO

1. Think back to the discussion of Canada's physical regions. Working in groups of four, pick four physical regions. Based on what you have learned about these regions, think of at least two exports for each. Give reasons for your choices. Then think of at least one import for each region. Again, give reasons for your choices. Present your results in an organizer, and share it with the class.

2. What goods might your community send to

    a) other communities?

    b) other provinces?

3. All families trade money for items that they want. What are some of the goods that you and your family have recently bought by "trading" money? List them in an organizer under the following headings: Clothes, Food, Other Manufactured Goods, Services. (Services are things that other people do for you, for example, shoe repair, dry cleaner, hairdresser/barber.)

Y ikes!" exclaimed Erin. "Some of those words on the board are really long. Do you think we're supposed to learn them?"

"I can hardly pronounce some of them," laughed Nathan. "But the word *parties* is in there, so there's got to be something fun about this!"

WHAT IS GOVERNMENT?

Government is a group of people who have been elected (chosen) by the people of a country. Their job is to make laws and to run the day-to-day activities that affect our lives.

Levels of Government

There are three main levels of government in Canada: federal, provincial or territorial, and municipal.

Federal

The federal (national) government is located in our capital city, Ottawa. It has many areas of responsibility that affect the whole of Canada, such as the armed forces and trade with other countries.

Provincial/territorial

Each province and territory has its own government as well. Some of its responsibilities are education, health care, and natural resources.

Municipal

Each city, town, or district has its own municipal (local) government. This level of government provides services such as police and fire protection, garbage removal, public transportation (bus and subway), and public libraries.

A LOOK AT PROVINCIAL GOVERNMENT

Each of the provinces/territories has its own government in its capital city. The provincial government meets in the legislature. In most provinces, it is called the **legislative assembly**.

Education

The provincial governments, along with local school boards, provide all of the funding (money) for teachers', secretaries', and custodians' salaries; textbooks and supplies used in the schools; and the building of new schools.

Highways

Provinces are responsible for building highways and maintaining them, including repairs and snow removal.

Health Care

In Canada, most of our medical bills (visits to the doctor and stays in the hospital) are paid for by the federal and provincial governments.

Justice System

In each province/territory, the laws are maintained by a system of courts and judges. (The federal government also has its own courts and judges to maintain federal laws.)

Tourism

Each province/territory makes sure that people from across Canada and throughout the

Different Names
The provincial legislature in Newfoundland is known as the House of Assembly. In Quebec, it is called the National Assembly.

Provincial Government

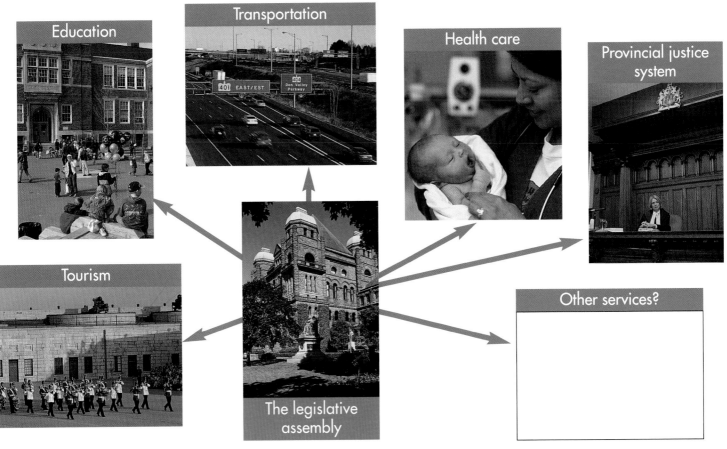

Education

Transportation

Health care

Provincial justice system

Tourism

The legislative assembly

Other services?

world are aware of the many attractions that it has to interest tourists. Tourists bring millions of dollars into Canada each year. In every province and territory, tourism is an important industry.

Provincial Taxes
Provincial governments spend *billions* of dollars each year to provide services such as education. The diagram below shows how they collect money to pay for these services.

This diagram shows us some of the services the provincial/territorial governments provide. What are some of the other services?

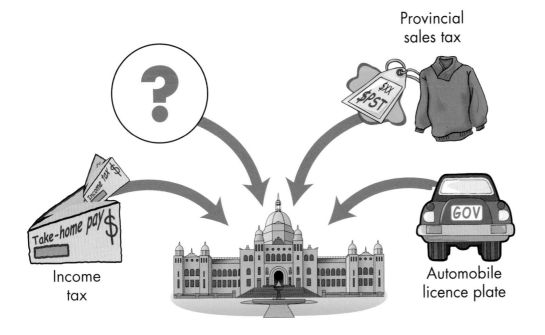

Provincial sales tax

?

Take-home pay $

Income tax

Automobile licence plate

*These are some of the ways that the provinces collect taxes. Provincial sales tax (PST): Most of the provinces put a **tax** on items that we buy, such as clothing, tools, lumber, and so on. Licence plates: The fees that drivers pay for new car licences or renewal stickers go to the provincial government. Income tax: Most workers pay part of their wages to the provincial government as income tax. Can you name another type of tax?*

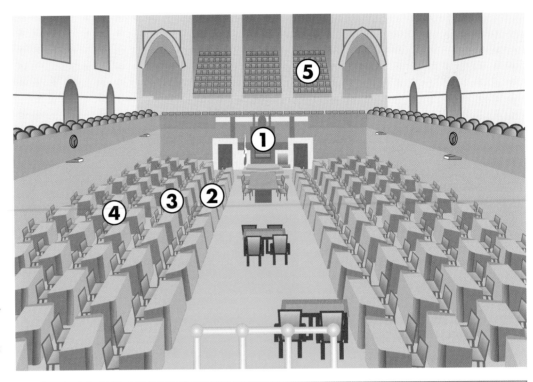

This is the inside of a typical legislative assembly building. For every riding in your province, there is one chair, or seat.

1 Speaker	**2** Premier	**3** Cabinet	**4** Members of Provincial Parliament	**5** Public Gallery

Different Titles

In Ontario, representatives of the provincial government are known as Members of Provincial Parliament (MPPs). In British Columbia, they are known as Members of the Legislative Assembly (MLAs); in Newfoundland, Members of the House of Assembly (MHAs); in Quebec, Members of the National Assembly (MNAs).

How Are Governments Chosen?

Approximately every four years, the people of each province/territory vote for a new government. On election day, they elect people who will be their representatives in government.

Ridings

Every province is divided up into areas called **ridings** so that each area of a province will have a representative in the government. Provinces have different numbers of ridings depending on their size and population. You live in one riding. Your cousin or friend who lives several kilometres away probably lives in another riding.

Each riding is allowed to elect one person to "sit" in the legislative assembly. One of these chairs, or **seats**, belongs to the representative in your riding.

Political parties

Political parties are groups of people who have the same ideas on how to run the government. Most provinces/territories have several political parties. Each party tries to win votes based on its ideas on how well it will run the province/territory.

Voting

On election day, voters are each given a ballot (a piece of paper) with the names of the people from each party. Voters place an X beside the person they would like to win the election.

The person with the most number of votes in a particular riding wins. The winner becomes the representative from the riding. She or he is now a **Member of Provincial Parliament (MPP)** and has a seat in the legislative assembly.

The party that has the largest

number of winning representatives forms the government.

How is the premier chosen?
The leader of the political party that has the largest number of winning representatives becomes the **premier** of the province.

How is the Cabinet chosen?
The premier is the most powerful person in the government. He or she chooses a number of MPPs from the party to form a **Cabinet**. Each member of the Cabinet is known as a minister and is in charge of a government department, for example, education. The premier and Cabinet make important decisions about the affairs of the province and make sure these decisions are carried out.

Who is the lieutenant-governor?
The **lieutenant-governor** is the queen's representative in the province. She or he must sign new laws before they can become effective. The lieutenant-governor is appointed by the prime minister of Canada. The position has little power and is largely ceremonial.

The Three Branches of Provincial Government
The legislative assembly is known as the *legislative* branch of government because it *legislates*, or makes, new laws.

The premier and Cabinet are known as the *executive* branch of government because it is their job to *execute* new laws (make sure new laws are put in place).

The judges and courts are know as the *judicial* branch of government because it is their job to *judge* that laws are applied fairly and accurately.

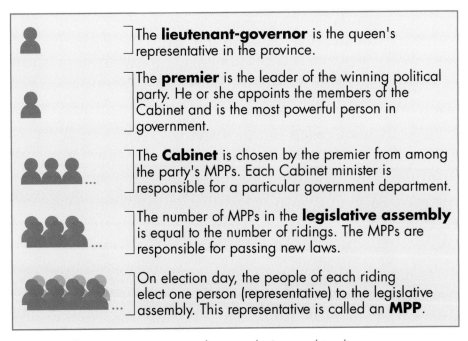

The **lieutenant-governor** is the queen's representative in the province.

The **premier** is the leader of the winning political party. He or she appoints the members of the Cabinet and is the most powerful person in government.

The **Cabinet** is chosen by the premier from among the party's MPPs. Each Cabinet minister is responsible for a particular government department.

The number of MPPs in the **legislative assembly** is equal to the number of ridings. The MPPs are responsible for passing new laws.

On election day, the people of each riding elect one person (representative) to the legislative assembly. This representative is called an **MPP**.

Provincial government at a glance—let's use this diagram to review what we have learned about provincial government.

SOMETHING TO DO

1. Who is your Member of Provincial Parliament? To which political party does she or he belong?

2. Who is the lieutenant-governor of your province? Find out more about the duties of the lieutenant-governor and report to your class.

3. How many ridings are there in your province? What is the name of the riding in which you live?

 symbol is a letter or picture that is used instead of a word or group of words. It gives important information to the reader. For example, an *x* in a math question is the symbol that tells you to multiply. A heart is a symbol for love. A flag is a symbol of a country.

On maps, a picture symbol stands for a real object and usually looks like that object. The symbols on this **pictorial** map of Canada give information about each province and territory. For example, a picture of tree with a tap and pail tells you that maple syrup is an important product of a province. A picture of an apple tells you that fruit is grown in a certain area.

With a partner, discuss what information the symbols in the map provide about each province and territory.

Arctic Ocean

Yukon Territory

Northwest Territories

Pacific Ocean

British Columbia

Alberta

Saskatche

Okanagan Valley

potash

SOMETHING TO DO

1. Choose two provinces or territories. Create a three-column organizer using these headings: Wildlife, Resources, Jobs. Using the information you have gathered from the map, compare the provinces/territories under each heading.

2. Using one of your choices in Activity 1, design a poster or brochure that will attract tourists to the province/territory.

3. Create a pictorial map of your school grounds. Use symbols to represent the features. For example, a picture of a swing or slide might represent the play area. Include a compass and a key (to explain your symbols).

etic North

Arctic Circle

avut

itoba

Hudson Bay

Québec

Newfoundland
and Labrador

L'Anse-aux-Meadows
(Viking Settlement)

Ontario

Prince
Edward
Island

Hibernia

The Grand Banks

New
Brunswick

Nova Scotia

Atlantic Ocean

0   300   600
kilometres

"The Rock"

POPULATION:
543 200

CAPITAL CITY:
St. John's

AVERAGE TEMPERATURE:
–4°C (January)
15°C (July)

PROVINCIAL FLOWER:
pitcher plant

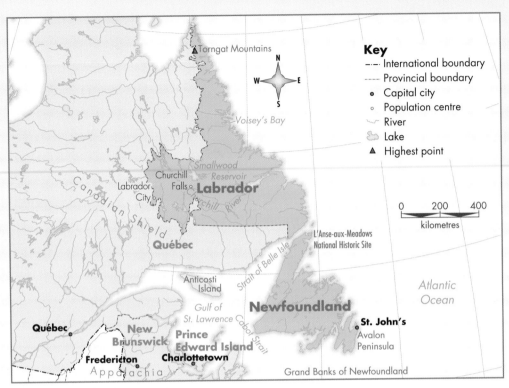

Key
– · – International boundary
- - - - Provincial boundary
• Capital city
○ Population centre
∼ River
🝖 Lake
▲ Highest point

0   200   400
kilometres

▲Torngat Mountains

Voisey's Bay

Smallwood Reservoir
Churchill Falls
Labrador City
Canadian Shield
Churchill River
Labrador

Québec

L'Anse-aux-Meadows National Historic Site

Strait of Belle Isle

Anticosti Island

Gulf of St. Lawrence
Newfoundland
Cabot Strait

Québec

New Brunswick
Prince Edward Island

St. John's
Avalon Peninsula

Atlantic Ocean

Fredericton
Charlottetown

Appalachia

Grand Banks of Newfoundland

The Atlantic puffin is Newfoundland's provincial bird. Puffins stuff themselves with small fish until they are almost too heavy to fly. North America's largest puffin colony is found in the bird sanctuary near St. John's.

Newfoundland is the largest of the four Atlantic provinces. It is also Canada's most easterly province. It is so far east that it has its own time zone, 30 minutes ahead of the rest of Atlantic Canada.

The province is made up of two parts. The smaller part is the island of Newfoundland, where most of the people live. The larger part, Labrador, is part of Canada's mainland and has fewer people. The Strait of Belle Isle divides the two parts. In northern Labrador, you can see the northern lights and the largest caribou herd in the world.

THE LAND
Newfoundlanders fondly call their province "The Rock." And most of it is! All of Labrador is in the Canadian Shield region and is rich in minerals. The rolling hills of the Appalachian Highlands spread over the entire island of Newfoundland. Both regions have thousands of lakes, large rivers, rocky beaches, ponds, bogs, and sand dunes.

THE CLIMATE
In the northern and western parts of Labrador, winters are bitterly cold. Temperatures can drop to –46 degrees Celsius. Corner Brook receives more than 381 centimetres of snow each year. Summer temperatures average only 10 to 15 degrees Celsius. In southern and coastal Labrador and the island, the ocean breezes keep the climate

moderate—not too hot or cold. Often, there is heavy fog around the coastal region.

RESOURCES AND INDUSTRY

Fresh Water

Tourists enjoy boating, swimming, and fishing in the province's fresh waters and along the seacoast.

The powerful water flow of the Churchill River in Labrador is used to generate electricity in hydroelectric plants along the shore. The plant at Churchill Falls produces enough electricity to supply all of Labrador's needs. It also sells some electricity to Quebec. The island has its own water and steam generation plants to supply its needs.

Forests

Almost half of the island is covered with large coniferous forests. These trees can grow in shallow, rocky soil. Most are **logged** (cut down) for pulpwood, which is processed into paper

products such as newsprint. Others supply lumber used to build houses and make furniture.

Minerals

While the island has most of the forests, mainland Labrador has most of the minerals, particularly iron ore. Large deposits are found near Labrador City and Wabush, the centres of the mining industry. The iron ore is shipped to other provinces. In Ontario, it is used in the **smelters** and steel mills

*Cape Spear is the most easterly part of North America. Built in 1835, the Cape Spear lighthouse is the oldest existing lighthouse in Newfoundland. It has become a **landmark**.*

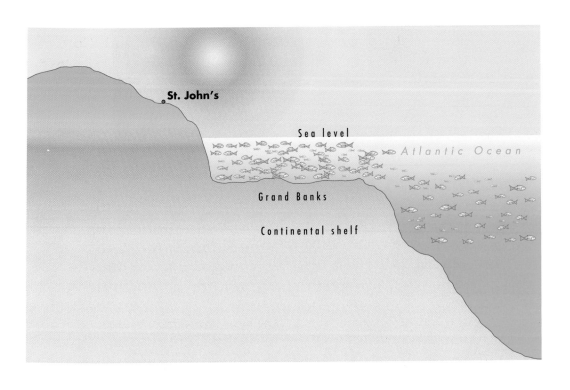

St. John's

Sea level

Atlantic Ocean

Grand Banks

Continental shelf

Minerals,
Seafood, Pork,
Paper products

Fruits and
vegetables,
Machinery,
Manufactured
goods

on the Great Lakes, such as those in Hamilton.

Fish

At one time, the Grand Banks teemed with fish, particularly cod. But **overfishing** reduced the size of the catches. In 1992, the federal government banned cod fishing until the cod are able to grow in number. Many fishers left their villages to find different jobs.

Other catches are salmon, lobster, crab, and scallops. Some of these catches are sold fresh. Most are taken to fish-processing plants, where they are cleaned, and then frozen or canned. Squid, capelin, and roe are exported to Japan and other Asian countries.

From the Arctic, it took three years for these icebergs to reach Notre Dame Bay. Here, they will melt in a matter of weeks.

SOMETHING TO DO

1. Part of Newfoundland's charm is found in its place names—Ha Ha Bay, Black Tickle, and Come by Chance are just a few examples. Using an atlas, locate other places with interesting names. On an outline map of Newfoundland, label these places. Display your map in class.

2. Newfoundland's pitcher plant grows in **peat bogs**. Research this unusual "meat-eater."

3. Research to find out why the Strait of Belle Isle is called "Iceberg Alley."

Prince Edward Island

"Garden of the Gulf"

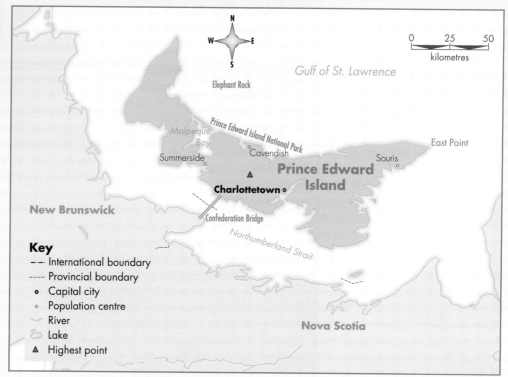

POPULATION:
136 200

CAPITAL CITY:
Charlottetown

AVERAGE TEMPERATURE:
–7°C (January)
19°C (July)

PROVINCIAL FLOWER:
lady's slipper

Prince Edward Island is Canada's smallest province, both in physical size and in population. Only the Arctic territories have fewer people. The province is often referred to as simply PEI.

THE LAND

PEI is an island that sits in the Gulf of St. Lawrence. It is separated from the rest of Canada by the Northumberland Strait. From the air it looks like a crescent moon, covered in neat patchwork fields of potatoes, golden grain, and green wooded areas. Crops grow so well in the rusty-red soil that the island is nicknamed the "Garden of the Gulf."

There are no mountains in PEI. In fact, the highest point of land is less than 150 metres above sea level. The land is best described as gently rolling.

Green Gables, a popular tourist spot, is the setting for the world-famous novel Anne of Green Gables, *by Lucy Maud Montgomery. The story has been translated into 15 languages and has twice been made into a movie.*

Sand dunes shaped by the wind and water protect the north shore of the island. Red- and white-sand beaches attract many people in summer. With its world-class golf courses and beautiful scenery, PEI is attracting more and more tourists.

THE CLIMATE

Prince Edward Island is surrounded by ocean. In winter, the water takes longer to cool. The winds from the ocean tend to make PEI's winter less cold than winter in the mainland provinces. However, the Strait of Northumberland freezes over for two or three months each winter, and snowfall averages over 300 centimetres.

In summer, the waters surrounding the island are warm enough to be enjoyed by swimmers. The average air temperature in July is a comfortable 19 degrees Celsius.

RESOURCES AND INDUSTRY

Fish

The sea has been a source of seafood from the time of the early settlers. Overfishing by both Canadian and foreign fishers has sharply reduced the numbers of fish, particularly cod. When the Canadian government banned cod fishing in 1992, the number of jobs available in the fishing industry declined. Today, lobster is the main catch of fishing fleets in PEI.

Many years ago, lobsters were so plentiful that farmers spread

Farmland

It is said that PEI has the richest soil in Eastern Canada. Its deep, fertile soil grows many kinds of crops. However, potatoes are by far the most important. PEI is often referred to as "Spud Island" (*spud* is a nickname for potato).

Potatoes are shipped across Canada and are exported to the United States, South America, and even Europe. But you may be surprised by the different forms these exports take. Most potatoes are exported for table use—to be peeled, cooked, and eaten. Some are shipped as seed potatoes—to be planted as crops. Many potatoes are first processed in local factories into potato chips and frozen french fries, and are then exported.

Farmers also grow wheat, barley, strawberries, raspberries, and blueberries. Most of the crops are sold locally.

them on their fields for **fertilizer**. Now, there are fewer lobsters. However, strict rules regarding the lobster **fishery** have prevented the lobster from suffering the same fate as the cod.

Lobster is a delicacy (a special treat) enjoyed by people the world over. Lobsters are shipped live in special containers to the rest of Canada and to other countries. Some lobster meat is canned or frozen in local factories and is then exported.

PEI is also well known for its other shellfish—oysters, scallops, and mussels.

Potatoes, Seafood

Electricity, Manufactured goods

Electricity

PEI's electricity is generated in oil-fired thermal plants. Some of it is brought in from New Brunswick by a submarine cable. The cost of electricity on the island is high. Recently, PEI has experimented with wind-powered generators, with some success. Maybe wind, which is clean and free, will be the province's "generator" of the future.

SOMETHING TO DO

1. Using the map scale on page 33 and a piece of string, estimate the length of PEI from one tip to the other. What observation can you make?

2. In 1997, PEI was joined to the mainland by the Confederation Bridge. The bridge has its own Web site. Prepare a report on this bridge to share with the class. If possible, include a photo.

3. You have just met Anne of Green Gables. Write a short story or dialogue that describes your meeting.

"Canada's Ocean Playground"

POPULATION:
936 100

CAPITAL CITY:
Halifax

**AVERAGE
TEMPERATURE:**
–5°C (January)
18°C (July)

PROVINCIAL FLOWER:
mayflower

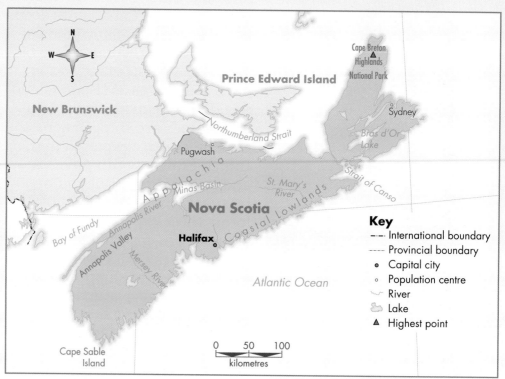

Key
- –·– International boundary
- ---- Provincial boundary
- • Capital city
- ○ Population centre
- ⌒ River
- Lake
- ▲ Highest point

"You have to use your imagination for my clues," said Sasha. "Picture land jutting out into the North Atlantic Ocean in the shape of a giant lobster. Listen to the bagpipe music. Watch the dancers stepping in time to the music. Smell the salt of the ocean."

"Good one!" said Ishwar. That's definitely Nova Scotia."

Nova Scotia is made up of two major parts: the mainland, which looks like the body of a lobster, and Cape Breton Island, which looks like the claws of a lobster. There are thousands of kilometres of coastline, with sandy beaches perfect for swimming, sailing, and fishing. No wonder Nova Scotians call their province "Canada's Ocean Playground"!

THE LAND
Nova Scotia has two physical regions: the Coastal Lowlands and the Appalachian Highlands. The Coastal Lowlands are on the northern part of the mainland. Bays, sandy beaches, and marshes make up the coastlines. The Appalachian Highlands run from southern Nova Scotia to Cape Breton's northern peninsula.

These young girls are performing a traditional Scottish dance at one of Nova Scotia's festivals. These festivals, along with historic sites, tides, coastal fishing villages, and hundreds of ocean beaches, attract thousands of tourists each year.

Visitors to Cape Breton Highlands National Park can view spectacular ocean scenery. The Cabot Trail, which follows two coastlines through this stunning setting, is the best way to see the park.

THE CLIMATE

Summer in the capital city of Halifax is pleasantly warm. Heavy fog often settles over the mainland and the coast. You might need to wear a jacket in the evenings because of the cool ocean breezes. The sea air keeps the coastal areas cooler during the summer and not as cold as the inland area during the winter. But rain, heavy snowfalls, and high winds, which batter the province, are the reasons Nova Scotia is called "the stormiest region of Canada."

These container ships are loaded and unloaded at Halifax, a key Canadian seaport. In the ice-free harbour, ships from all over the world can be seen year-round.

DID YOU KNOW?

Nova Scotia exports about 9 million Christmas trees each year.

Agricultural products, Seafood, Wood products, Christmas trees, Industrial minerals, Tires

Food and beverages, Oil, Natural gas, Machinery

RESOURCES AND INDUSTRY

Forests

Most of the province is covered in rich softwood forests of spruce and fir trees. Softwood is ideal for making pulp-and-paper products such as your notebook. These trees also supply lumber and plywood, which are used in the building of homes.

Fish

In the past, Nova Scotia was known for its many fish. A **continental shelf** close to the shore was an ideal spawning and feeding ground for a wide variety of fish. As in the other Atlantic provinces, these large fish stocks have been reduced because of overfishing. Many fishers and workers in fish-processing plants have been put out of work.

Lobsters, snow crabs, scallops, mussels, and herring are valuable catches. Some lobster and snow crab are sold fresh. Some are canned or frozen in fish-processing plants.

Aquaculture, the raising of fish in tanks, ponds, or reservoirs, is a new, growing industry. Salmon, trout, and mussels are raised on these "fish farms."

Farmland

The Annapolis Valley, in the fertile crescent on the south side of the Bay of Fundy, is well-known for its apple orchards and dairy farms. Vegetables and dairy, poultry, and pork products are sold locally in Nova Scotia. Apples and dairy products are sold to other provinces and to the United States.

Minerals

Nova Scotia has rich deposits of industrial minerals such as gypsum, sand, gravel, and rock salt. These resources are mined for use in construction material to build houses, skyscrapers, and everything in between.

Coal is a hard, black mineral that is formed from the remains of plant life. Burning coal is a source of energy. Nova Scotia has enough coal deposits to generate most of its electricity. A few small hydroelectric plants provide the rest.

SOMETHING TO DO

1. Write your own legend describing how you think wild horses arrived on Cape Sable Island.

2. Research the details of the Halifax Explosion in 1917. Write a newspaper article describing this tragedy as you think it might have been written in 1917.

"The Picture Province"

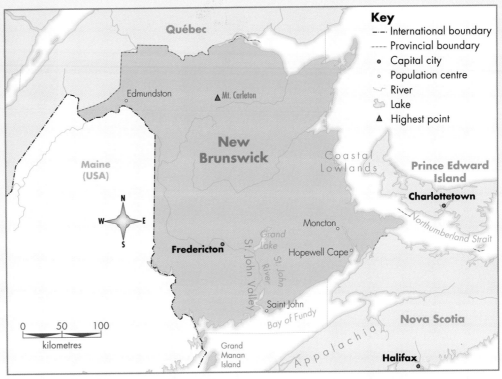

Key
- –·– International boundary
- ---- Provincial boundary
- • Capital city
- ○ Population centre
- ⌐ River
- 𝄞 Lake
- ▲ Highest point

POPULATION:
751 400

CAPITAL CITY:
Fredericton

AVERAGE TEMPERATURE:
–10°C (January)
19°C (July)

PROVINCIAL FLOWER:
purple violet

"Are they the highest tides in Canada or in the whole world?" asked Samantha.

"In the whole *world*!" exclaimed Erin. "Twice a day, the tides rush in to the Bay of Fundy, rising as high as a five-storey building. Then they drain back into the ocean, and rush in again when the tide turns. It's awesome!"

New Brunswick, the largest of the three Maritime provinces, borders on Nova Scotia, Quebec, and United States. It is the only officially **bilingual** province. This means that all provincial government services, such as education, must be offered in two languages: English and French.

THE LAND
The rolling hills of the Appalachian Highlands are in the central and eastern part of the province. They are mostly covered in thick forests and beautiful lakes and streams.

Along the Northumberland coast are spongy marshes, sand dunes, and beaches.

THE CLIMATE
The weather is changeable. Usually, the summers are pleasantly warm inland, while the winters are cold and snowy. The sea air keeps the coastal areas cooler during the summers and not as cold as the inland areas during the winters. Heavy snowstorms often hit the southern coast.

French Canadians in New Brunswick
The French created a settlement near Port-Royal in 1604. It was one of the earliest permanent European settlements in North America. Eventually, New Brunswick came under British rule, but French people continued to keep their language and culture. Today, about one-third of the population of New Brunswick is French Canadian.

At Hopewell Cape, you can stand on the ocean floor at low tide and see rocks shaped like flowerpots. At high tide, the water flows over the flowerpots.

High and Low Tides

Tides are caused mainly by the gravity (pull) of the moon on the earth's oceans. As the moon circles the earth, it pulls the oceans back and forth. When this movement of water, at its highest point, reaches land, it is called high tide. When the water moves away from the land, it is called low tide.

RESOURCES AND INDUSTRY

Forests
New Brunswick is one of the most heavily forested regions in the world. Most of the softwood trees that are logged are sent to pulp-and-paper mills to be made into paper products such as newsprint. Some of the trees are used for lumber to make furniture.

Minerals
Northern New Brunswick has mineral deposits of iron ore, tin, lead, copper, silver, and zinc. Near Sussex, there are deposits of potash and antimony. Potash is used mainly for fertilizer. Antimony is added to lead to increase its hardness and strength.

Farmland
Only a small portion of the land is suitable for farming. Potatoes, particularly seed potatoes, are grown in the northern Saint John Valley. Some are canned or processed as frozen french fries. Potatoes and their products are the province's main food export.

Dairy farms are found mainly in the south. The dairy-processing industry provides milk products such as butter and cheese.

Fish
The main fishing areas are the Gulf of St. Lawrence, Northumberland Strait, and the Bay of

Pulp-and-paper products, Christmas trees, Minerals, Potatoes, Dairy products

Wheat, Hydro-electricity, Manufactured goods

No wonder thousands of tourists visit New Brunswick each year! Boardwalks twist over fragile marshland where plants and wildlife can be seen. Lakes and thick forests lure hunters and fishers. Coastal villages, tides, reversing falls, and historic sites are just a few of many attractions.

Fundy. As in the other Atlantic provinces, overfishing has reduced the number of fish. However, there are still good catches of lobster, crab, and herring. The fish are sold fresh or sent to processing factories. Many New Brunswickers work in these factories, freezing, canning, salting, or smoking the fish for export.

Aquaculture, or fish farming, is a thriving industry in New Brunswick. Atlantic salmon are raised in large, nylon-mesh floating cages in waters along a protected coastline.

SOMETHING TO DO

1. In groups of four, brainstorm the advantages and disadvantages of boardwalks over a fragile **ecosystem**. Be prepared to share your final answers with the class.

2. Using the library or the Internet, research aquaculture. Find out about the different types of containers used. How and where are they used?

3. Research the ostrich fern. Why do you think this plant was chosen to be on New Brunswick's coat of arms?

"La belle province" ("The Beautiful Province")

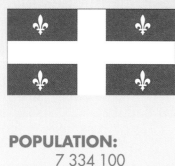

POPULATION:
7 334 100

CAPITAL CITY:
Quebec City

AVERAGE TEMPERATURE:
–12°C (January)
18°C (July)

PROVINCIAL FLOWER:
madonna lily

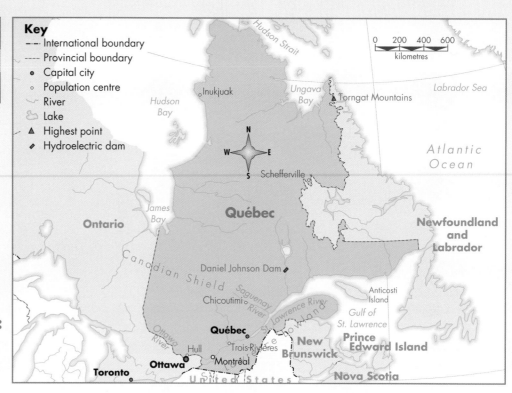

Key
- –·– International boundary
- ---- Provincial boundary
- ● Capital city
- ○ Population centre
- ∿ River
- ☁ Lake
- ▲ Highest point
- ◆ Hydroelectric dam

Signs in Quebec are written in French because it is the official language of the province.

"*Ça va*, Erin?" Spencer asked, while cutting out a picture of *Bonhomme*.

"*Ça va bien!*" replied Erin. "Wow! It looks like you're going to the Winter Carnival in Quebec City. You'll get to see the famous ice sculptures and the night-time parades."

"Yes!" said Spencer. "And I'm planning to speak French the whole time I'm there."

"*Bonne chance!*" Erin wished Spencer, as she moved toward the doorway.

Spencer quickly reached for his French dictionary. "*Bonne* what?" he asked.

PARLEZ-VOUS FRANÇAIS?

Good for Spencer! He'll have fun trying out his French in Quebec. But he doesn't have to worry if he gets stuck on some words. Although Quebec is the only province where French is the official language, there are many English-speaking Quebeckers.

Also, many Quebeckers are bilingual, so they can speak both French and English.

The French were the first Europeans to start a permanent settlement in Quebec in 1608. Later, when Quebec came under British law, many French-speaking people continued to

live there. That is why today most of the people are French Canadian. Their language, traditions, and culture set Quebec apart from the other provinces.

Quebec is by far the largest province in Canada. It is larger than Alaska, which is the biggest state in the US. In fact, Quebec is larger than most countries in the world. It has the second highest population of all Canada's provinces. Most Quebeckers live near the St. Lawrence River, in the area between Montreal and Quebec City.

THE LAND

Quebec has three physical regions: the Canadian Shield, the St. Lawrence Lowlands, and the Appalachians.

The Canadian Shield spreads over most of the province and has rich mineral deposits. Thick forests and thousands of beautiful lakes and rivers blanket most of the land.

As you travel to the far north of Quebec, you'll notice that the **vegetation** lessens and becomes smaller as the land becomes flat, wet, and boggy. This is the Arctic tundra. Polar bears and caribou live here.

The St. Lawrence Lowlands extend in a narrow band along both sides of the river. This region of Quebec has the best climate and soil conditions for farming. Hundreds of dairy farms are found here. It is the smallest of the three regions, and the most populated.

The Appalachians are part of a mountain chain in eastern North America. The Appalachian region of Quebec is on the south bank of the St. Lawrence River, between the Richelieu River and the Gaspé peninsula. It has some good farmland, many coniferous trees, and rich mineral deposits.

THE CLIMATE

Average Temperatures

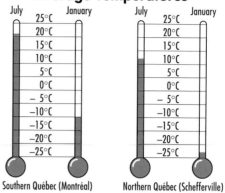

Southern Québec (Montréal)   Northern Québec (Schefferville)

Average Snowfall

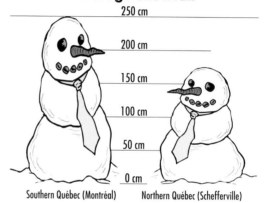

250 cm
200 cm
150 cm
100 cm
50 cm
0 cm

Southern Québec (Montréal)   Northern Québec (Schefferville)

In January 1998, southern Quebec and eastern Ontario were hit by the worst freezing-rain storm in recorded history. It has become known as the Great Ice Storm.

Look at the thermometers. What is the difference between the average summer and winter temperatures in northern and southern Quebec? As a class, measure 175 cm and 250 cm on the classroom wall. Using this information, describe Quebec's climate.

RESOURCES AND INDUSTRY

Fresh Water

Quebec is known for its countless lakes and rivers. These attract tourists for boating, fishing, swimming, and other activities. The St. Lawrence River is the province's most important waterway. The seaway allows ocean-going ships to reach the Great Lakes.

Quebec is a world leader in producing hydroelectricity. The largest hydroelectric project in Canada is located in the James Bay area. The province provides all its own electricity needs and also sells electricity to Ontario, New Brunswick, and the United States.

Forests

Quebec has the second-largest area of forestland in Canada. In the fall, these mixed-wood forests of fir, spruce, pine, maple, oak, and ash trees display spectacular leaf colours.

Most of the softwood trees that are logged are sent to pulp-and-paper mills. Here, they are processed into paper products, particularly newsprint. Quebec's pulp-and-paper industry is one of the largest in the world. Some trees are sent to furniture-making factories. Others are used for lumber to build houses.

Many of the maple trees are tapped, and the sap is processed into maple syrup. Thousands of Quebec's evergreen trees are sold yearly as Christmas trees in other provinces and in the United States.

The logging camps, sawmills, pulp-and-paper mills, and furniture factories provide thousands of Quebeckers with jobs.

Farmland

The most fertile land lies along both sides of the St. Lawrence River. Although dairy farming takes place throughout Quebec, most dairy farms are found on the south shore of the

The pulp-and-paper industry along the Saguenay River is one of the most important in Canada.

St. Lawrence, between Montreal and Quebec City. Milk from the farms is collected as fresh milk and industrial milk (to be made into cheese, cream, powdered milk, and other products). Quebec produces more dairy products than any other province and ships them across the country. Second to dairy farming is crop growing—mostly grain crops to feed farm animals.

Minerals

Quebec is the world's leading producer of asbestos. It also produces all of Canada's titanium, which is used in the paint industry. Over one-quarter of Canada's gold is mined in Quebec, as are copper, zinc, and iron. There are also deposits of industrial minerals such as peat, limestone, silica, granite, and mica.

| Hydroelectricity, Minerals, Forest products, Dairy products, Auto parts |
| Manufactured goods, Oil, Natural gas, Wheat |

Asbestos is a grey, threadlike mineral that is not affected by fire or chemicals. Also, it does not conduct electricity. After its fibres (threads) are separated out and cleaned, they can be woven. Asbestos is used to make heat-resistant clothing. It is added to cement to strengthen it.

J.A. Bombardier of Valcourt, Quebec, was the inventor of the snowmobile.

When You Visit There . . .

• **Quebec City** is North America's only walled city north of Mexico. This "split-level" city is divided into Upper Town and Lower Town. To get from Lower to Upper Town, you can walk up the Champlain stairs. Or take the easy way . . . on an outdoor elevator.

Winters are fun in Quebec City. People, ski, skate, toboggan, snow-shoe, and ice fish. Each February, Bonhomme Carnaval welcomes visitors from all over the world to the Quebec Winter Carnival. There are even daring canoe races among the ice floes in the St. Lawrence. In spring, people head off to a cabane à sucre (sugar shack) for sugaring off.

Quebec City celebrates summer, too. The streets are alive with musicians, jugglers, and artists, especially in the old part of the city. Hundreds of kilometres of safe bicycle paths are perfect for touring. Every year, there is a music and arts event known as Festival d'été (Summer Festival).

• **Montreal** is Canada's second-largest city, and the world's second-largest French-speaking city. Located on an island in the St. Lawrence, it has one of the largest and busiest seaports in Canada.

When it's cold and stormy, Montrealers can head to their underground city. Shops and walkways beneath Place Ville-Marie bustle with people. Along the harbour is Old Montreal, an area of narrow cobblestone streets with old buildings. You can hear the "clip-clop" of horses' hooves as they draw sightseers in calèches. Many people find that the combination of French and British roots make Montreal a unique and lively city.

In Old Montreal, you can visit historical buildings, watch the street performers, or rollerblade at the old port.

Quebec City's Lower Town has some of North America's oldest buildings. Upper Town, perched on bluffs, is the modern section.

Every year, more than 1 million skiers hit the Laurentian and Appalachian slopes in Quebec.

SOMETHING TO DO

1. With a string, measure the province of Quebec from (a) north to south and (b) east to west. Using the map scale on page 42, find these approximate distances in kilometres.

2. Using "Climate" as your title, write a short paragraph describing Quebec's climate. You can find information in the diagram on page 44.

3. In an organizer, compare Labrador and Quebec under the headings "Minerals" and "Energy."

4. Using an outline map of Quebec and an atlas, follow the directions below:

   a) Draw the provincial boundary lines of Quebec.

   b) Label the neighbouring provinces.

   c) Label the major bodies of water around Quebec.

   d) Using a different colour for each, colour and label the three physical regions of Quebec.

   e) Label the following: Gaspé, Quebec City, Montreal, and the St. Lawrence River.

"The Heartland of Canada"

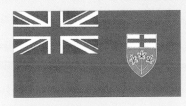

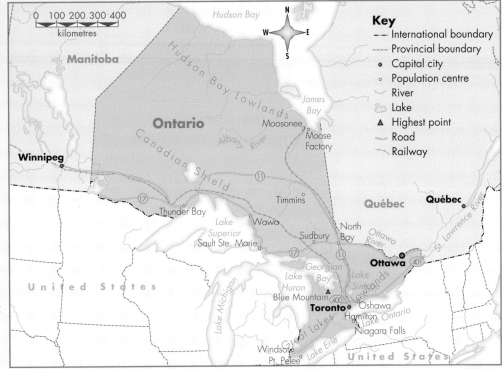

0 100 200 300 400 kilometres

Key
- -·- International boundary
- ---- Provincial boundary
- • Capital city
- ○ Population centre
- River
- Lake
- ▲ Highest point
- Road
- Railway

POPULATION:
11 404 800

CAPITAL CITY:
Toronto

AVERAGE TEMPERATURE:
–5°C (January)
21°C (July)

PROVINCIAL FLOWER:
trillium

"You come face to face with the falls," said Sasha. "There's a tunnel that lets you see the falls from behind." "It's unbelievable!"

"Bet you got soaked to the skin from the mist," said Shivon, laughing. "There's about 155 million litres of water falling every *minute*!

Did you guess that Sasha and Shivon were talking about Niagara Falls?

From the exciting hustle and bustle of the big-city streets to the silence of the wilderness in the north, Ontario has a lot to offer. It's a great place to see any time of the year.

Ontario gets its name from a Huron word that means "sparkling water." It is Canada's most populated and second largest province. The province stretches from Manitoba's border east to the Ottawa River, and from the icy shores of Hudson Bay south to the Great Lakes.

Northern Ontario is home to many types of wildlife.

THE LAND

Ontario is often considered to have two distinct regions—Northern and Southern Ontario—which are divided at Lake Nipissing. Find Lake Nipissing on the map.

Northern Ontario

Northern Ontario has two physical regions: the Hudson Bay Lowlands and the Canadian Shield. The Hudson Bay Lowlands region is a flat, marshy wilderness that surrounds the bay. It is the home of many species of birds, polar bears, beaver, and other wildlife.

The Canadian Shield is a wide area of rock, forest, and thousands of lakes and rivers that offer some of the best hunting and sport fishing in North America. Although the soil is poor, making farming difficult, there is a wealth of forests and minerals.

Northern Ontario has 90 per cent of the province's land but only 10 per cent of the population.

Southern Ontario

Much of Southern Ontario is covered by the Canadian Shield. However, the Great Lakes Lowlands extend from the Ottawa River to Lake Huron. This region includes all of south-eastern Ontario and contains some of the richest farmland in Canada. Nine out of ten Ontarians call this region home.

Northern Ontario's Cities

The main cities are located on the original railway line built in the 1800s. North Bay is a transportation centre. Sudbury is the heart of the mining district and the northern centre for medicine and communications. Sault Ste. Marie is an important steel producer, and Thunder Bay is a major port on Lake Superior. Find these cities on the map.

The Terry Fox Memorial stands just outside Thunder Bay. It was here that Terry Fox had to stop his heroic walk because cancer had spread to his lungs.

Cottage Country

About an hour's drive north of the Great Lakes is Ontario's "cottage country." Here, in the southernmost part of the Canadian Shield, thousands of Ontarians "venture forth," attracted by the many lakes and deep forests. During the weekend, highways are busy as people drive to cottages to get away from the rush of life in the city.

This is Ouimet Canyon near Thunder Bay. Northern Ontario has some of the most spectacular scenery in Canada.

Few places can beat the beauty of fall in "cottage country."

Southern Ontario—Something for Everyone

Don't be surprised to find yourself sharing the road with a horse-drawn Mennonite buggy in St. Jacobs, near Waterloo. Or you might be standing at the top of the CN Tower (the world's tallest structure), overlooking Toronto and Lake Ontario. Perhaps you might enjoy a Shakespearean drama performed on the stage in Stratford. Near Peterborough, you might be awed by the petroglyphs (stone carvings) made by the Ojibwa people 500 to 1000 years ago. There are plenty of interesting activities for people who visit or live in Southern Ontario.

DID YOU KNOW?

Point Pelee on Lake Erie is the most southerly part of Canada's mainland. It is as far south as northern California.

THE CLIMATE

Ontario has a wide range of climates. In the spring, before the ice has cleared from the rivers and shorelines of Hudson Bay, snowdrops, crocuses, and even apple blossoms have begun to bloom in Southern Ontario.

Southern Ontario's climate is moderated (made less harsh) in winter by the winds off the Great Lakes. Since water takes longer to cool than land, the Great Lakes seldom freeze over. Hudson Bay is much farther north, so it freezes over each winter. It has little moderating effect on Northern Ontario's climate. Looking at the chart, compare the January and July temperatures of these regions. What is the difference in July? in January?

Average Temperatures		
	July	January
Hudson Bay	15° C	–25° C
Toronto	21° C	–5° C

Areas that receive westerly winds from the Great Lakes, such as Parry Sound and Sault Ste. Marie, are called the "snowbelt." They generally get over 250 centimetres of snow each year, while Toronto gets less than 150 centimetres.

RESOURCES AND INDUSTRY

Minerals

In the late 1800s, the railway was being built through Northern Ontario. The workers who were blasting the rock discovered the rich minerals of the Canadian Shield. Deposits of gold, silver, copper, nickel, and uranium were uncovered. Small mining towns sprang up throughout the north country. But minerals do not always mean prosperity for communities. They can be very much in demand one year but not the next. Today, many of these towns still experience "boom or bust" years.

We know how important minerals are to factories in the manufacturing of goods. It was the rich minerals of Northern Ontario that helped the province become the manufacturing centre of Canada.

Forests

The fall colours of Northern Ontario's trees are famous the world over. The forests are often a mix of coniferous (pine, spruce, cedar) and **deciduous** (maple, oak, birch, elm) trees. They are home to moose, deer, elk, wolf, and fox, as well as dozens of species of birds.

Ontario's logging industry produces pulp and paper, lumber, and plywood. These products are shipped to Southern Ontario and to the United States. Almost all of Ontario's forests are owned by the provincial government. Private companies are given licences to cut timber.

Farmland

Southern Ontario has most of Canada's best soil, making agriculture an important industry in the province. Ontario usually ranks first among the provinces in the value of the crops grown. Farmers grow a wide variety of crops, corn being the largest. It is used mainly as **fodder** (food) for cows, hogs, and chickens. Certain varieties are sold as food for people.

Some farmers prefer to specialize (grow just one or two crops). In the Niagara region, with its rich soil and warm climate, some farmers only grow fruit, such as peaches or grapes. Holland Marsh, southwest of Lake Simcoe, was once under water. Gradually, over many years, the water was drained, leaving a rich, black soil, ideal for growing vegetables. Each summer, farmers from Holland Marsh sell their fresh vegetables at open markets across Southern Ontario.

Dairy farming is the most common type of farming. Throughout Canada, only Quebec produces more dairy products.

This dam at Niagara Falls provides hydroelectric power for much of Ontario and New York State.

Fresh Water

Even without the Great Lakes, Ontario has a lot of water. The many lakes and rivers, in both Northern and Southern Ontario, offer leisure-time activities such as fishing and canoeing.

As well, many rivers are used for the production of hydroelectricity. Niagara Falls is one of the largest producers of electricity in Canada. It provides electricity for both Ontario and the United States.

Manufacturing

Ontario is Canada's leading province in manufacturing. This means it has the most factories, in which many different goods are produced.

Transportation

From the days of the early pioneers, Upper Canada (Ontario) was the place to settle. Land was either free or very reasonable, and the Great Lakes provided a natural highway. Adjoining rivers led settlers inland. Gradually, roads were built along the shores of the Great Lakes and to inland communities. Better transportation attracted more people. By the early 1900s, Southern Ontario had the largest population in Canada. It was filled with bustling communities, large and small.

Today, Ontario has a network of super highways and railways. Trucking is a rapidly growing industry. Thousands of trucks deliver goods across Ontario each day.

Location

Ontario is fortunate because of its location in the **heartland** (centre) of Canada. Businesses in Ontario trade goods with the Prairie provinces in the west, and with Quebec and the Atlantic provinces in the east. Just a few kilometres to the south, across the Great Lakes, is Canada's biggest trading partner, the United States.

Many of the manufacturing factories are located in what is known as the "Golden Horseshoe." This region curves

DID YOU KNOW?

Dr. Roberta Bondar was Canada's first female astronaut. She spent eight days in orbit aboard the shuttle *Discovery*. Dr. Bondar was born in Sault Ste. Marie.

Manufactured goods, Farm products, Minerals, Wood products, Pulp and paper

Oil, Natural gas, Minerals, Seafood products

ucts that we use every day are made from steel.

Automaking

In 1904, the Ford Motor Company started an automobile company in Windsor. In 1907, the McLaughlin Motor Car Company started in Oshawa, and later became General Motors of Canada. Since that time, automobile manufacturing has been an important source of **employment** (jobs) for the people of Ontario. Today, five companies have automaking plants in Ontario. Many other companies make auto parts: tires, windshields, plastic dashboards, bumpers, and so on. Automaking is Ontario's *most important* industry.

The frozen Rideau Canal becomes a 7-kilometre skating rink each winter. Thousands of skaters enjoy the scenic outing in the centre of Ottawa. The Parliament Buildings can be seen in the distance.

in the shape of a horseshoe around the northern and western shores of Lake Ontario—from Oshawa to St. Catharines—and includes Toronto and Hamilton. Almost one-half of Ontario's population lives here. The word *golden* suggests that it is a very rich part of Canada.

Steelmaking

Hamilton and Sault Ste. Marie are the largest steelmakers in Ontario. The steel is made from iron ore that is mined in Labrador. The iron ore is mixed with limestone, coal, and scrap iron. These materials are then smelted into a hot, molten liquid. Small amounts of other minerals are added. When it is cooled, the result is pure steel. Many prod-

Steelmaking is one of Canada's most important industries.

THREE ONTARIO COMMUNITIES

Mining Community

The huge "Big Nickel" towers over the city of Sudbury in Northern Ontario. The Sudbury basin contains one of the world's largest and richest deposits of copper and nickel ore. Today, it produces almost one-third of the world's nickel.

Sudbury ships nickel and copper across Canada and the world to manufacturers that use these minerals to make many different products. Stainless-steel knives and forks are examples of products made of steel that contains nickel.

Located in the rocky Canadian Shield, Sudbury has the natural resources for mining, but very poor soil for farming. The city must depend on farming communities to provide most of its fruits and vegetables.

A Farming Community

Peaches, sweet cherries, pears, plums, grapes—welcome to the Niagara Fruit Belt! This farming community produces about three-quarters of Canada's peaches and almost all of Canada's grapes.

Some of this "tender" fruit is sold in local fruit markets, while the rest is shipped to communities in Ontario, other provinces, and other parts of the world. The area also boasts a thriving wine industry.

The fruit belt lies in the Great Lakes Lowlands region. It has excellent soil and the perfect climate for growing fruit. But this region must depend on manufacturing communities to provide it with products such as automobiles, stoves, and refrigerators.

An Industrial Community

"A City in Motion" is the sign that welcomes visitors to Oshawa. It is the home of General Motors of Canada, which manufactures automobiles and ships them across Canada and the United States. Oshawa produces automobiles, but relies on other communities to provide the **raw materials** needed, such as steel, plastic, and rubber. As well, much of the fruit in the Oshawa markets comes from the Niagara region.

As you can see, no community can provide everything it needs. Your community uses some goods that are manufactured or grown in another community. Can you think of something your community might send to other places in Ontario?

If you visit the Niagara Fruit Belt during the growing season, you'll see fruit blossoms everywhere.

The 9-metre-tall "Big Nickel" is the perfect symbol to welcome you to a mining community.

These cars were manufactured at the General Motors plant in Oshawa. They will be shipped across North America.

The CN Tower, glass skyscrapers, and the Skydome make Toronto's skyline easily recognizable.

TORONTO

Toronto began as a small town in 1793. It was named York by Lieutenant-Governor John Graves Simcoe. At that time, it consisted of a few dirt streets, some wooden sidewalks, and a small population. During the spring thaw and periods of rain, it earned the nickname "Muddy York."

Today, Toronto is the largest city in Canada and the capital of Ontario.

Tourism

Each year, more than 20 million people visit Toronto. It is the number-one tourist destination in Canada. To accommodate these visitors, Toronto has almost 8000 restaurants and over 30 000 hotel rooms. Its English theatre district is the third largest in the world, after London, England, and New York City. North America's largest underground shopping area connects many hotels and office towers, including 1000 stores and restaurants.

The People

Toronto's population is almost 2.5 million. One-third of the population of Canada lives within 160 kilometres of Toronto!

DID YOU KNOW?

The people of Toronto have more cell phones per capita (for each person) than any other North American city.

This is a scene of "Muddy York," with its wooden sidewalks and horse and buggies. As a class, compare Muddy York to a modern city.

These scenes show some of the many peoples who contribute to Toronto's multicultural society.

One-half of the population of the United States lives within a day's drive.

In 1997, Canada received 80 000 immigrants. A large number came to Ontario, particularly Toronto. Toronto has more people from different countries than any other city in Canada.

Over 80 different languages are spoken in Toronto. One-third of the people of Toronto speak a language other than English at home.

Asia –	**647 165**
Africa –	**85 475**
Europe –	**560 930**
Great Britain –	**158 070**
Caribbean and Bermuda –	**155 730**
Central and South America –	**122 320**
United States –	36 355
Other –	**6 860**

This pie chart shows the place of birth of 1 772 905 immigrants who were living in Toronto in 1996. Each "slice," or segment, represents the number of immigrants from a particular region of the world.
Source: Data from Statistics Canada, 1996 Census.

SOMETHING TO DO

1. Compare the population of Toronto to that of Prince Edward Island. Make two statements about your findings.

2. On a blank sheet of paper, place the names of Sudbury, Niagara, Oshawa, and your community in each corner. Using arrows and labels, indicate products that each community exchanges with the others. Share your results with the class.

3. Using the map scale on page 49, estimate the distance from Toronto to Sudbury.

4. Working with a partner, volunteer to find out more about the Group of Seven. Report to your class.

5. Using the pie chart of immigrant populations in Toronto, list each place of birth from largest number of immigrants to smallest. Beside each place of birth, list the number of immigrants. Make two general statements about what you observe.

DID YOU KNOW?

Toronto is referred to as "Hollywood North" by the movie industry. Many movies and television programs are filmed here. In fact, Toronto ranks third in North America for both TV and film production.

"The Keystone Province"

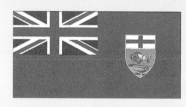

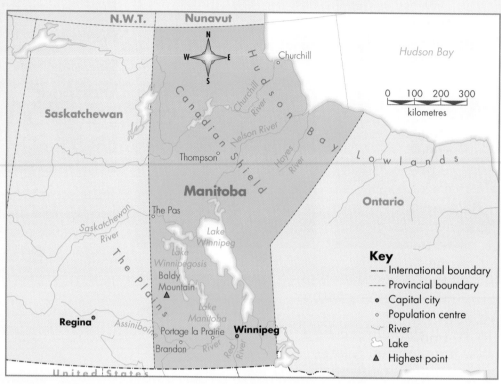

POPULATION:
1 141 000

CAPITAL CITY:
Winnipeg

AVERAGE TEMPERATURE:
–18°C (January)
20°C (July)

PROVINCIAL FLOWER:
prairie crocus

Manitoba is the easternmost of the three Prairie provinces. It is known as the **keystone** province because of its location in the centre of Canada.

Manitoba lies at Canada's transportation crossroads. Manufactured goods shipped from Eastern Canada to the Western provinces pass through Winnipeg. Because of its large railway and highway systems, Winnipeg is called the

Teddy bears? Not on your life! Tourists flock from around the world to see Churchill's most popular attraction . . . from a safe distance. The port of Churchill on Hudson Bay is known as the "Polar Bear Capital of the World." Each year, dozens of polar bears gather along the shores to hunt for seals. White beluga whales can often be seen in the summer feeding at the mouth of the Churchill River.

"Crossroads of Canada." Wheat and other farm products are shipped from the prairies through Winnipeg to Eastern Canada and other parts of the world.

THE LAND

Manitoba has three main physical regions. The northern part of the province is covered with the rock, lakes, and forests of the Canadian Shield. It is rich in minerals, and home to the black bear, moose, and caribou.

Only one-fifth of the land is prairie. This is the southern part of Manitoba, where the main cities of Winnipeg and Brandon are surrounded by rich farmland.

The rest of the province is the Hudson Bay Lowlands—frigid, almost treeless land, dotted with wet, spongy wetlands called **muskeg**.

THE CLIMATE

Look at the chart below.

Average Temperatures		
	July	January
Winnipeg	20° C	–18° C
Churchill	12° C	–28° C

What general statement can you make from this information?

The most **precipitation** (rain and snow) falls in the south during the summer (about 50 centimetres). However, Winnipeg enjoys an average of 2000 hours of sunshine each year. It is one of Canada's bright spots.

RESOURCES AND INDUSTRY

Fresh Water

Like many Canadian provinces, Manitoba has many lakes and

Winnipeg sits at the junction of the Assiniboine and Red Rivers. In the spring, if the winter snow melts too quickly, it is a recipe for disaster.

The Fresh-Water Fishery

Manitoba's lakes provide jobs for fresh-water fishers. They catch whitefish, pike, walleye, sauger, trout, and other species. After the fish are filleted and processed, they are ready for market. Almost half the catch is exported to the United States.

Minerals, Electricity, Farm products, Fish

Manufactured goods, Seafood products

Muskeg is the breeding ground for hundreds of animal and birds and millions of insects such as mosquitoes and black flies.

rivers. In fact, there are over 100 000 lakes, many of which have never been named. Lake Winnipeg is the largest. It is no wonder that Manitoba's most important resource is fresh water. Besides attracting hunters, fishers, and trappers, it is the most important source of hydroelectric power on the prairies. Manitoba exports electricity to the other Prairie provinces and to some states in the US.

Farmland

The fertile prairie land is a source of a variety of crops, including wheat, barley, and oats. By far, the most important is wheat. Farming is an important industry and a major source of employment for the people of Manitoba. The province is the largest producer of flaxseed,

sunflower seeds, and canola in Canada. These are pressed into cooking and salad oils. The oil in your salad dressing may very well have come from Manitoba.

The Red River Valley in southern Manitoba has the longest **growing season** in the province. (This is the period of the year when it is continuously warm enough for crops to grow.) Farmers here specialize in growing sunflowers, sugar beets, and other vegetables for canning.

Minerals

The mineral-rich Canadian Shield contains minerals such as nickel, copper, zinc, and gold. Thompson is one of most northern towns in the province. It has one of the largest mining industries in North America, and accounts for all of Manitoba's nickel production.

SOMETHING TO DO

1. Thompson is an important mining town. It has its own Web site. Find out more about Thompson. Describe your findings in an organizer under the following headings: Location (use latitude and longitude), Climate, People, Industry/Jobs. Share your organizer with the class.

2. Research why Manitoba is called the "Keystone Province." Share your findings with the class.

3. Using your atlas, find the source of the Red River. What did you discover?

Saskatchewan

"The Breadbasket of Canada"

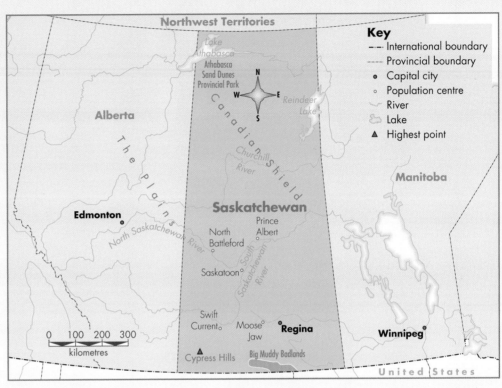

Key
- –·– International boundary
- ---- Provincial boundary
- ● Capital city
- ○ Population centre
- River
- Lake
- ▲ Highest point

POPULATION:
1 025 600

CAPITAL CITY:
Regina

AVERAGE TEMPERATURE:
–18˚C (January)
18˚C (July)

PROVINCIAL FLOWER:
western red lily

Saskatchewan is the middle province of the three Prairie provinces. Unlike all the other provinces, most of its boundaries are not determined by rivers, lakes, coasts, or mountain ranges, but by latitude and longitude. Saskatchewan's name comes from the Cree word *kisiskatchewan*, which means "swiftly flowing river."

Kernel

What is wheat? It is a tall grass with small kernels at the top. When it is ripe, the kernels are separated from the rest of the plant and ground into flour.

THE LAND

There are two main physical regions. The Canadian Shield extends over the northern half of the province. This low, rocky land is covered with forests and lakes and is rich in minerals.

To the south lie the prairies (often called "the plains")—flat, fertile land that seems to stretch forever. Deep river valleys cut through the centre of the prairies. Most of the province's cities and towns are scattered across the prairies.

THE CLIMATE

Saskatchewan has cold winters and hot summers. Winter temperatures of –50 degrees Celsius and summer temperatures of 40 degrees Celsius have been recorded.

Climate is very important to the wheat farmers. First, they need the right amount of rainfall—not too much, not too little. They also need a long growing season. Frost can kill new plants in the spring and damage fully grown plants in the fall.

From the grain elevators, the wheat is loaded onto trains and shipped across Canada and to many other countries.

RESOURCES AND INDUSTRY

Farmland

Saskatchewan's most important natural resource is its soil. Almost half of Canada's farmland is in Saskatchewan. If you fly across the province in summer, it looks like one huge wheat field.

Wheat is Saskatchewan's most important crop. The province produces over 54 per cent of the wheat grown in Canada. It is harvested and delivered to grain elevators, where it is tested for quality. The highest-quality wheat is made into flour, which in turn is made into bread, pasta, and breakfast foods. Lower-quality wheat is used as fodder. The higher the quality, the more the farmer is paid.

Farmers also grow oats and barley as fodder for their cattle. Canola and sunflowers crops are pressed into salad and cooking oil.

DID YOU KNOW?

Athabasca Provincial Park is remarkable because it has sand dunes that are 30 metres high. Sand dunes are not found so far north anywhere else in the world.

Oil and Natural Gas

Saskatchewan's other natural resources are found beneath the soil. Recently, rich deposits of oil and natural gas have been discovered. Oil is refined into gasoline to fuel cars and trucks and to heat homes and businesses. Natural gas is also used to heat buildings.

Wheat, Oil, Potash

Manufactured goods, Electricity, Seafood products

Saskatchewan

Today, there only a few thousand buffalo living in protected parks.

Where the Buffalo Roam

Long ago, before the arrival of the Europeans, the number of buffalo that roamed through the Prairie provinces and the United States was thought to be nearly 50 million. Aboriginal peoples living on the plains hunted the buffalo on horseback. The skins were used for clothing, blankets, and homes (tepees), and the bones for tools and utensils. Even buffalo dung was used for fires. The fur traders ate a mixture of buffalo meat and fat, known as pemmican.

As more Europeans arrived to explore and settle the land, space for the buffalo decreased. Large numbers of buffalo were killed. Huge quantities of buffalo bones were sent to the United States to be made into fertilizer.

Many years ago, what is now the capital city of Regina was known as "Pile O' Bones" because so many buffalo were killed there. Their bones were left to dry in the sun.

Potash

Saskatchewan has enough of the mineral called potash to last for hundreds of years. Potash is used in the making of fertilizer. Some people add fertilizer to the soil to increase growth in their lawns and gardens.

SOMETHING TO DO

1. Research how wheat in the field becomes spaghetti on your plate. Report your findings to the class.

2. Research the early history of the RCMP. Prepare an oral (spoken) presentation for your class.

3. Using an atlas, work in groups of four to name the latitudes and longitudes that form most of Saskatchewan's borders. Compare your answers.

4. As a class, discuss the meaning of the phrase "Breadbasket of Canada."

"The Princess Province"

POPULATION:
2 913 400

CAPITAL CITY:
Edmonton

AVERAGE TEMPERATURE:
−13°C (January)
18°C (July)

PROVINCIAL FLOWER:
wild rose

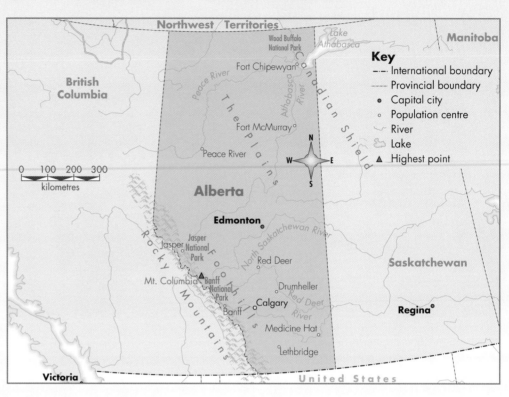

Dinosaurs roamed the prairies millions of years ago. Their skeletons have been found in Dinosaur Provincial Park, near Drumheller. Dinosaur Trail is a 50-kilometre drive through the site where the dinosaur fossils were discovered. Nearby, Tyrrell Museum has one of the largest displays of dinosaur skeletons in the world.

"I didn't know they once had dinosaurs in Alberta!"

Alberta is the farthest west of the three Prairie provinces. It shares many of the same physical features with its eastern neighbours, Saskatchewan and Manitoba.

Alberta is called "The Princess Province" because it was named after Princess Louise Caroline Alberta, daughter of Queen Victoria.

THE LAND
Alberta has three main physical regions. The foothills and the

Rocky Mountains rise in majestic splendour along the southwest border with British Columbia.

In the northeast corner of the province lies a small section of the Canadian Shield. This region of ancient rock is rich in minerals such as gold, nickel, and copper.

The remainder of Alberta, and by far the largest area, is the prairie, or the plains. It is generally flat or gently rolling land, sometimes cut by deep river valleys. Coyotes, deer, and foxes wander freely through the open prairie. Forest grows over much of the northern prairie. The rest is covered by rich fertile soil that is excellent for farming.

THE CLIMATE

The distance from southern Alberta to the northern border is over 1200 kilometres. The weather from north to south can be quite different. Winters are long and cold everywhere in the province, but more severe in the north. About 60 centimetres of precipitation fall in the foothills compared to only 45 centimetres in the rest of the province.

However, there are surprises. Occasionally each winter, a warm, dry wind from the Pacific Ocean slips through the mountains. These winds are called chinooks. They can raise the temperature by as much as 20 degrees Celsius in a few hours. As a result, the snow melts and it becomes a spring day. It's time for a barbecue or a game of golf. In a day or two, winter returns with all its fury.

The city of Banff is one of Canada's most famous resort towns, noted for its skiing and scenery.

RESOURCES AND INDUSTRY

Farmland

Crops are grown throughout most of the prairie. Wheat is by far the most important crop. It is used to make flour, a key ingredient in bread and pasta. Barley and oats are grown as fodder for the farmers' livestock (cattle and horses).

Farms and ranches are spread over more than one-third of the land. With so much wide, open space and plenty of fodder, Alberta has more beef cattle than any other province. When the cattle are ready for market, they are shipped to meat packers. There, the beef is processed and shipped to markets across North America and as far away as Japan, China, and Russia.

Oil and Natural Gas

Far beneath the surface of the Alberta plains are large deposits (pockets) of oil and natural gas. The Athabasca Tar Sands in

Alberta is the land of cowboys and cowgirls wearing Stetson hats and boots. They look after millions of beef and dairy cattle on the huge, rolling plain.

Oil, Natural gas, Beef, Wheat

Manufactured goods, Seafood products, Farm machinery

northern Alberta is one of the largest deposits of oil in the world.

Oil and natural gas provide energy-hungry Canada with its gasoline and heating needs. Natural gas is moved across Canada in large pipelines. It is distributed in almost every province to provide heating for homes and businesses. Some gas is piped to the United States.

Alberta provides most of Canada's oil and natural gas, which, in turn, bring in a lot of money for the people and government of Alberta. Alberta is one of Canada's richest provinces. No wonder oil is often called "black gold!"

Wells are drilled deep into the earth to find deposits of oil.

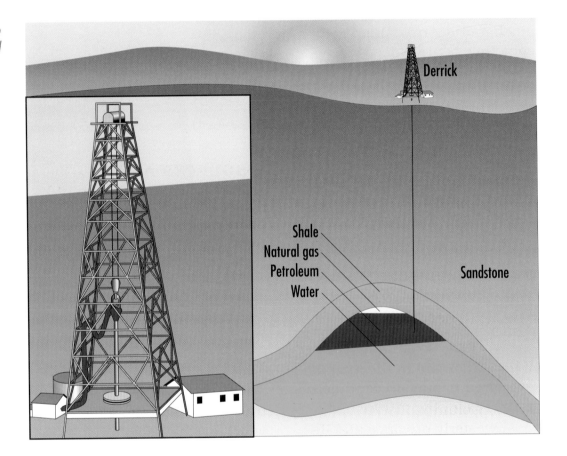

Derrick

Shale
Natural gas
Petroleum
Water

Sandstone

SOMETHING TO DO

1. Use the map on pagees 10–11 to answer the following:

   a) Which direction is Alberta from Ontario? from the Yukon?

   b) Two provinces, one territory, and one country border Alberta. Name them.

2. Canada is one of the highest users of energy (electricity, oil, gas, natural gas) in the world. Think, pair, and share to brainstorm why this is so. From your ideas choose two main reasons.

3. Is oil or natural gas used in your community? Find out how it is delivered from Alberta. Report to your class.

British Columbia

"Beautiful BC"

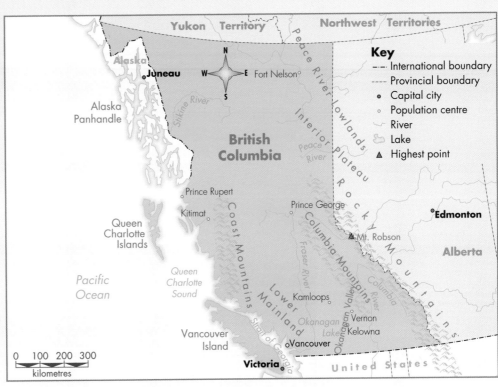

POPULATION:
4 014 300

CAPITAL CITY:
Victoria

AVERAGE TEMPERATURE:
–0°C (January)
18°C (July)

PROVINCIAL FLOWER:
Pacific dogwood

"There are lots of topics on British Columbia to choose from, you know," said Rishi. "Of all the provinces, British Columbia has the biggest and oldest trees, the most varieties of bats, and the most types of animals. What topic did you choose?"

"I'm *totally* into totem poles," said Erin.

British Columbia is Canada's most westerly province and its third largest. British Columbia is part of the Western Cordillera, a chain of mountains that extends up the west coast of North America. BC, as it's often called, is best described as a land of contrasts.

THE LAND
British Columbia has three main mountain ranges: the Coastal, the Columbia, and the Rocky Mountains, all of which extend from north to south. Between the Coastal and the Columbia Moun-

tains are the Interior Plateau and the Okanagan Valley.

Find the Rocky Mountain Trench in the diagram on page 68. It is the longest valley in North America, stretching the entire length of BC. The Columbia, Fraser, and several other rivers have their sources here. They gradually wind their way through deep cuts in the mountains to the Pacific Ocean.

At the mouth of the Fraser River, where it finally reaches the ocean, is the only flat area along the coast. This area is called the Lower Mainland. It contains rich

"Hole in the Sky" is the oldest standing totem pole in the world. The totem poles outside many of the homes of the coastal Aboriginal peoples had symbols that described the groups who lived there.

This is a profile of the Western Cordillera, from the Pacific Ocean to Alberta.

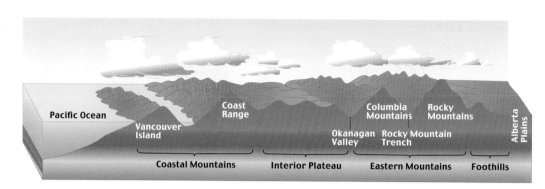

British Columbia is a land of natural beauty. Attracted by snow-capped mountains, thick rain forests, rushing rivers, rolling pastures, and lush farms, many people move to BC each year.

farmland and BC's largest city, Vancouver.

Vancouver Island and the Queen Charlotte Islands lie to the west, protecting the mainland from the Pacific storms. These islands are actually the top of an underwater mountain range that stretches north to Alaska. Victoria is located on Vancouver Island. More than 70 per cent of BC's population lives in or around the cities of Vancouver and Victoria.

In the northeast are the Peace River Lowlands. Here, the Peace River has its source and makes its way across Alberta to Lake Athabasca.

The northwest is a vast wilderness with few roads and little population. It is cut off from the coast by the Alaska panhandle, which belongs to Alaska (United States).

THE CLIMATE

Sunshine, rain, snow, cold winters, mild winters—British Columbia's climate has something for everyone. Like its physical features, BC's climate has wide variations. Two main features affect the climate in BC: the ocean and the mountains.

The Ocean

Warm, moist winds blow in from the Pacific Ocean all year long. The climate on the coast is warm and wet. The ocean temperature changes very little. The water keeps the air cool in the summer and warm in the winter. Victoria's winters are the warmest of any city in Canada.

The Mountains

As the warm, moist air reaches the mountains, it is forced to rise into cooler air. The cooler air releases the moisture in the form of rain and snow.

up the mountains, the rainfall increases to over 300 centimetres. Farther up the mountains, the moisture falls as snow. Victoria may experience a winter with no snow at all.

Find the Interior Plateau in the diagram below. You can see that the air from the Pacific first passes over two sets of mountains—Vancouver Island and the Coastal Range—before it reaches the plateau. The air is

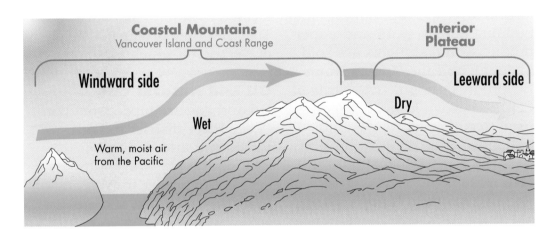

As the air passes over the mountain and down the leeward side (away from the wind), it is warmed and holds whatever water it has. The leeward side of the mountains are very dry. This same process takes place over each of BC's mountain ranges.

Precipitation

The windward side (facing the wind) of Vancouver Island in some places receives as much as 400 centimetres of rain in one year. The city of Victoria, which is on the leeward side, receives on average less than 100 centimetres.

Vancouver's rainfall varies. At the airport, which is right on the coast, the rainfall is about 100 centimetres a year. Twenty-five kilometres inland and part way

now very dry. The Interior Plateau and Okanagan Valley receive only 25 centimetres of precipitation a year.

The Frost-Free Season

The **frost-free season** on the coast averages about 200 days, the longest in Canada. However, in the Interior Plateau it averages only half this number. The ocean breezes keep the coast relatively warm in winter. For the rest of BC, it's a different story. In January, the plateau may have temperatures of –20 degrees Celsius. In the north, it is much colder.

This warning for schoolchildren was published in the Kitimat newspaper. Find Kitimat on the map. It is located at higher elevation than Victoria and much farther north. It may get as much as 10 metres of snow each year!

WARNING: Do Not Touch the Hydro Wires When Climbing Snowdrifts.

A lot of rain, fertile soil, and a long growing season produce these giant trees. They include Douglas fir, red cedar, and Sitka spruce. Some trees grow more than 90 metres high and are hundreds of years old.

RESOURCES AND INDUSTRY

British Columbia has plenty of natural resources. Forestry, mining, energy, and fishing account for most of BC's exports, and together provide most of the jobs in the province.

Forests

Almost two-thirds of BC is forested, and logging is the most important industry.

Most products made from the forests are exported. Lumber for building homes, pulp-and-paper products, and shingles are sold to Japan and the United States. BC produces about two-thirds of Canada's sawn lumber, which is used to construct homes and buildings.

Minerals

The Cariboo Gold Rush started it all. In the 1850s, gold was discovered along the Fraser River and in the Cariboo Mountains. Thousands of miners flocked to the interior to find their own "pot of gold."

Today, minerals are BC's second most important resource. Gold, coal, copper, asbestos, zinc, and lead are mined throughout BC and are exported across Canada. Coal is shipped to Japan where it is used by the steel industry.

Fresh Water

BC's many steep and rugged rivers provide the necessary power to generate hydro-electricity. Power plants are located in several locations in BC. Together they produce a surplus of electricity, which is exported.

Oil and Natural Gas

Oil and gas are piped from the Peace River district to both Vancouver and Vancouver Island. The pipeline continues across the border to Washington State where the oil and gas are sold.

Fish

In the mid-1990s, the fishing industry employed over 25 000 people, including fishers and the

The fallers cut the trees into logs. They are then tied together in log booms and taken to the closest mill.

Saving the Environment

Forests are valuable for reasons other than industry. They produce the oxygen that we need to breathe, and provide a home for many birds and animals. Many people in BC are concerned about how fast the forests are disappearing. They think that fewer trees should be logged. But people who work in the logging and pulp-and-paper industries worry about their jobs disappearing. These are difficult choices. Making sure that the forests survive is a concern for everyone.

Mining companies, too, have to keep an eye on the environment. Recently, the provincial government has refused to allow mining in several areas where there is concern for plant and animal life.

DID YOU KNOW?

British Columbia has a large fleet of ferries that takes people and cars up and down the coast and to BC's many islands.

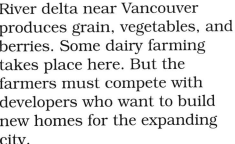

Lumber, Paper, Minerals, Salmon, Oil, Natural gas, Fruit

Manufactured goods, Farm products

people who worked in canning and fish-processing plants. Fishing contributed several hundred million dollars to the economy.

The most important catch is the five species of Pacific salmon. Salmon return from the ocean to their spawning rivers, where they complete their life cycle. As they gather at the river mouths, they are caught in huge numbers by large, modern fishing vessels. This method has seriously reduced the number of fish and threatens the industry. The fishers and the government are trying to find a way to stop the decline in the numbers of fish.

Farmland

Farming is a small but important part of the economy. The Fraser River delta near Vancouver produces grain, vegetables, and berries. Some dairy farming takes place here. But the farmers must compete with developers who want to build new homes for the expanding city.

Fish ladders are used to help salmon get around human-made objects such as dams for hydro plants. However, in some places spawning has been significantly reduced.

SOMETHING TO DO

1. Use an atlas to find the precipitation levels for Prince Rupert, Toronto, Halifax, and Iqaluit. Show this information in a bar graph. Make two general statements about your results.

2. Choose one of the following topics to research:

   a) the life cycle of the Pacific salmon

   b) methods of logging in British Columbia

   c) British Columbia's ferry service

   d) the bats of British Columbia

"The Land of the Midnight Sun"

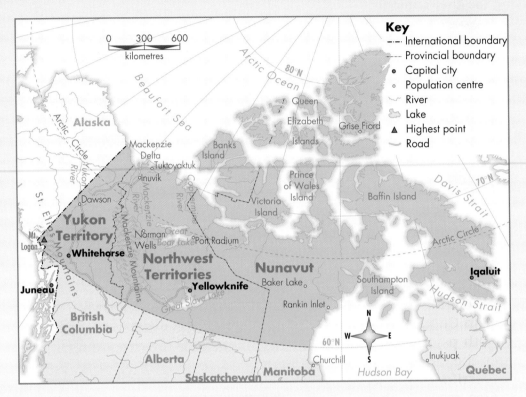

Yukon Territory

Northwest Territories

Nunavut

	Yukon Territory	Northwest Territories	Nunavut
POPULATION:	13 600	42 000	25 000
CAPITAL CITY:	Whitehorse	Yellowknife	Iqaluit
AVERAGE TEMPERATURE:	–27°C (January) 12°C (July)	–28°C (January) 16°C (July)	–30°C (January) 11°C (July)
TERRITORIAL FLOWER:	fireweed	mountain avens	purple saxifrage

The Land of the Midnight Sun lies above the Arctic Circle. During the month of June, there are 24 hours of sunlight each day. The sun never sets. In December, the opposite happens. The sun never rises. It is dark all day. Can you imagine going to school when it feels like the middle of the night?

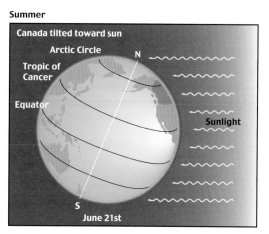

Summer

Canada tilted toward sun

Arctic Circle

N

Tropic of Cancer

Equator

Sunlight

S

June 21st

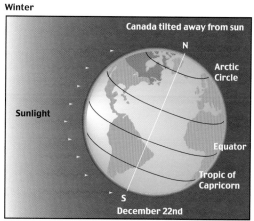

Winter

Canada tilted away from sun

N

Arctic Circle

Sunlight

Equator

Tropic of Capricorn

S

December 22nd

In June, the earth is tilted toward the sun. All the land in the Arctic Circle receives sunlight for 24 hours each day. In winter, the opposite happens. The earth is tilted away from the sun. There is no sunlight in the Arctic Circle during December.

As a class, find the 60th parallel of latitude on the map on pages 10–11. "North of 60" refers to all the land in Canada that is north of the 60th parallel of latitude. It includes the three territories: Yukon Territory, Northwest Territories, and Nunavut. Together, they make up over a third of Canada's land area but have a very small fraction of its population.

Winter
Ground is frozen.

Permafrost

Summer
Top layer melts.

Active layer

Permafrost

During the winter, the ground remains frozen. In summer, the warm sun melts the top few centimetres. This is called the "active layer."

THE LAND

North of 60 is an immense region of ice, snow, rock, and mountains. The mountains are mainly in the Yukon. They are part of the Western Cordillera that extends up the west coast of Canada.

Much of the remainder is rocky, barren land known as tundra. No trees grow in the tundra because of the intense cold and poor soil. **Permafrost** extends across the whole area. Permafrost is frozen ground that never entirely melts. In the summer, the top layer is warmed by the sun and thaws, but it is not able to drain away because of the frozen ground beneath. The result is wet, soggy ground.

Permafrost causes problems

An Inukshuk is an Inuit trail marker. It is built by piling stones in a form that looks like a person. It is used as a sign post to help guide travellers across the barren northern land.

During the summer, is plenty of sunlight, even at midnight. These residents of Frobisher Bay are playing a midnight baseball game.

The Dancing Northern Lights

In the late winter, the northern skies often glow with the northern lights. The changing red, green, and blue colours move up and down as if they were dancing. The northern lights have sparked the imaginations of people for centuries. Although best seen in northern Canada, the northern lights are sometimes seen in southern Canada on cold, clear winter nights.

Wildlife

North of 60 is home to thousands of species of birds and animals. Each summer, birds arrive from all across North America to breed, then they return south in the early fall. Surely, Arctic terns get the most "air miles." They arrive each summer from the Antarctic, only to return in the fall.

Animals such as the caribou, polar bear, and muskox are full-time residents. They wander across the frozen landscape in search of food.

for builders. The heat from homes and paved highways causes the permafrost to thaw. Roads begin to sink and homes begin to lean to one side. Because of these problems, some homes are built above the ground on posts. Pipes inside utilidors (protective covering) carry water and heat into the homes and take sewage out. Roads are built on gravel ridges to prevent damage by permafrost.

THE CLIMATE

Winters are long, dark, and cold. Temperatures of –40 degrees Celsius are not uncommon. Summers are the opposite. Long days and plenty of sunshine often push temperatures into the teens. Some people even swim in the Arctic Ocean on a warm, sunny afternoon. Brrrr!

A "desert" in the Arctic? Little precipitation (less than 30 centimetres) falls in much of the territories, so the whole area officially can be called a desert. But melted permafrost does create swamps known as muskeg.

RESOURCES AND INDUSTRY

Fresh Water

The territories contain one-quarter of all the fresh water in Canada. Thousands of lakes and rivers cover the entire area. In the summer, they serve as highways for boats and, in the winter, for snowmobiles and sleds.

The largest river system in Canada is the Mackenzie. It starts at the Slave River in northern Alberta, flows to Great Slave Lake, and tumbles 3000 kilometres to the Arctic Ocean.

Many species of wildlife inhabit the lakes and rivers. Hunters and fishers from around the world visit the North for a chance to try their luck. Other tourists come to enjoy the beautiful northern scenery. Tourism is becoming increasingly important in the territories.

Minerals/Oil and Natural Gas

Much of the territories is covered by the rocky Canadian Shield. Geologists (people who study rock) estimate that the territories contain just about every type of mineral known to humans. Important discoveries of gold, zinc, copper, and uranium have been made. Since the late 1800s, minerals have played an important role in the lives of the local people.

Several oil and natural gas fields have been found along the Mackenzie River. Small amounts of oil and natural gas are exported. However, there are problems with transporting these resources:

- The large populations of people who use minerals, oil, and natural gas live too far away. The cost of transporting these materials is too high.

*When the Mackenzie River reaches the Arctic Ocean, it slows down, allowing all the **silt** and gravel it is carrying to settle to the bottom. Gradually, over thousands of years, these islands were formed. Can you find the main channel of the river?*

Oil, Natural gas, Minerals, Aboriginal art

Fresh food, Dairy products, Manufactured goods

- Nature's balance in the North is very delicate. For example, it takes a tree several years to grow a few centimetres. The building of highways and pipelines would cause damage both to plant life and the movement of caribou each year.

Minerals, oil, and natural gas are the most important natural resources in the territories. When safer and cheaper methods of transportation are found, their importance will increase.

The Klondike Gold Rush
In 1896, gold was discovered on Bonanza Creek in the Yukon. That same year, thousands of people rushed to "stake their claim." In the next few years, they took out about $100 million worth of gold.

The Métis
Métis are people of both Aboriginal and European backgrounds.

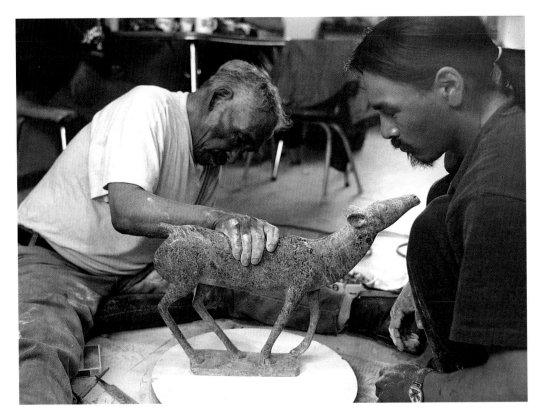

Aboriginal art is very popular. Carvings from stone and whalebone, drawings, and clothing are sold throughout Canada and the world.

Aboriginal Peoples
A large number of the people who live in the territories are Aboriginal peoples. They are the original inhabitants of Canada, and include First Nations and Inuit. First Nations refers to organized groups of Aboriginal peoples who live in Canada. There are hundreds of First Nations in Canada: for example, the Mi'kmaq in the Maritimes, the Ojibwa in Ontario, the Plains Cree in Saskatchewan, and the Haida in British Columbia.

North of 60 there are two First Nations: the Gwich'in in the Yukon and the Dene in the Northwest Territories.

Inuit are Aboriginal peoples who live above the treeline in Nunavut and in northern Quebec and Labrador.

Nunavut ᓄᓇᕗᑦ

Nunavut, Canada's newest territory, was created on 1 April 1999. Nunavut means "Our Land" in Inuktitut, the language of the Inuit. Eighty per cent of the residents are Inuit.

Nunavut has 20 per cent of Canada's land area, almost 70 per cent of its coastline, but just a tiny per cent of its population. There are only 28 small villages spread across this large expanse of land.

Iqaluit, the capital, is the largest village.

There are no permanent roads in Nunavut. All-terrain vehicles or snowmobiles are used for short distances. To travel from one village to another, there is only one choice—flying. Residents take airplanes to travel long distances, much the same way we take trains or buses. If people become seriously ill or have an accident, they are flown to the nearest hospital.

On 1 April 1999, shortly after midnight, the people of Nunavut celebrated the creation of their new territory.

SOMETHING TO DO

1. In pairs, make a bar graph that compares the populations of Canada's provinces and territories. Make three general statements about your observations.

2. Find out more about Robert W. Service. Volunteer to read a favourite part of one of his poems.

3. Iqaluit is the capital of Nunavut. Research Canada's newest capital, using the following headings as a guide: Location, Weather, Language, People, Schools, Festivals, Wildlife. Report your findings.

Glossary

Aboriginal peoples descendants of Canada's first inhabitants.

Antarctic the region around the South Pole.

aquaculture the raising of fish in tanks and ponds.

Arctic the region around the North Pole.

bilingual able to speak two languages.

branch an offshoot of a river.

Cabinet a group of elected people who advise the premier of a province.

canal a human-made waterway used for water transportation.

capital city the location of the government for each province and territory.

cardinal points the four main points of the compass—north, south, east, and west.

cartographer a person who makes charts or maps.

coniferous a tree with needle leaves and cones.

continent one of the large pieces of land on the earth's surface.

continental shelf the gentle slope of the ocean bottom from the shore to deeper water.

coordinate the number and letter given to a grid point on a map.

deciduous a tree that sheds its leaves in autumn.

delta land at the mouth of a river made up of silt deposited by the river.

dune a low hill of sand in desert areas or on the seacoast.

eastern hemisphere the eastern half of the earth.

ecosystem the way in which people, animals, and plants work together in the environment.

electricity a form of energy generated by friction.

employment to work for pay or a salary.

energy a resource that helps us do work (for example, food for people, gasoline for cars).

equator the 0-degree line of latitude that circles the earth.

erosion the gradual wearing away of land or rock by natural forces.

export to send goods or produce out of a country.

fertilizer materials added to the soil to enrich it and help plants and crops grow.

fishery the part of the sea (or other body of water) where fishing is carried on.

flood plain the level valley floor on either side of a river that is flooded during periods of heavy rain or melting snow.

flow the continuous movement of water.

fodder food for horses, cattle, and sheep (for example, corn).

founding peoples the first groups of people to settle in a country.

frost-free season the period of time between the last frost in the spring and the first frost in the autumn.

generator a machine that produces electricity.

glacier a massive ice sheet formed during the Ice Age.

grid horizontal and vertical lines on maps used to locate places.

groundwater water that sinks into the earth and is absorbed into the soil and the solid rock beneath the soil.

growing season the period of the year when the weather is continuously warm enough to grow plants.

heartland refers to the centre of Canada.

horizontal going across from left to right.

hydroelectricity electricity produced by water power.

immigrant a person who has left his or her country to live permanently in another country.

import to bring in goods or produce from another country.

industry the business of making manufactured goods.

intermediate points the in-between points of the compass—northeast, northwest, southeast, southwest.

key the part of a map that explains the symbols used in the map.

keystone the stone at the top of an arch that locks the other stones in place.

landform a natural feature of the earth's surface (for example, a mountain).

landmark an outstanding or elevated object marking a particular place.

latitude (lines of) imaginary horizontal lines drawn on a map above and below the equator.

legend a key explaining symbols found on a map.

legislative assembly a group of people elected to govern in a particular province.

lieutenant-governor the queen's representative in a province.

lock an enclosure in a canal, with a gate at each end, that allows vessels to pass from one level to another.

log (*verb*) to cut a tree into logs.

longitude (lines of) imaginary lines drawn on a map running from the North Pole to the South Pole.

meander a curve in a winding river.

Member of Provincial Parliament (MPP) a person elected to provincial government.

(BC, Quebec, and Newfoundland use different terms—see page 26.)

meridian of longitude a line of longitude.

mouth where a river or stream enters a larger body of water.

multicultural made up of people of many different races, religions, and cultures.

muskeg large areas of swampy land.

natural resource something produced by nature that is useful to people (for example, trees).

North Pole the point on the earth's surface that is as far north as possible.

northern hemisphere all of the land and water north of the equator.

overfishing catching more fish than nature can replace.

oxbow lake the large curve in a river that is eventually cut off from the rest of the river to form a lake.

parallel of latitude a line of latitude.

peat bog a large, damp area where decayed plant material forms sponge-like earth, which is sometimes used for fuel.

permafrost ground that is frozen year round.

pictorial illustrated with pictures rather than words.

plain a large, flat or gently rolling area of land.

political map a map that shows borders, cities, roads, rivers, and lakes.

political party a group of persons who have the same ideas about governing a province, territory, or country.

precipitation rainfall or snowfall.

premier the government leader in a province.

prime meridian the 0-degree line of longitude that runs from the North Pole to the South Pole.

province one of the political areas into which Canada is divided.

raw material a resource in its natural state.

region an area sharing similar characteristics such as landscape or climate.

riding an area that elects one representative to government.

river a body of water that flows from higher ground into another body of water.

seat a place where the elected representative from a certain riding sits in the government.

silt a deposit of mud or fine soil from running or slow-moving water.

smelter a furnace where raw materials are heated in the process of making steel.

source where a river begins.

South Pole the point on the earth's surface that is as far south as possible.

southern hemisphere all of the land and water south of the equator.

spawn to lay eggs (refers to fish, frogs, toads, and shellfish).

stream water carried by a river or a creek.

stream bed the bottom of a river over which the water flows.

tax money collected from people and businesses to pay for government services.

territory one of the political areas into which Canada is divided.

trade to buy, sell, or exchange things.

tributary a stream or river flowing into a larger river or lake.

tundra a large, treeless plain in the Arctic regions.

turbine a machine or motor driven by a flow of water, steam, or gas.

vegetation all plant life including trees, plants, grasses, and so on.

vertical something that is straight up and down.

waterfall a stream or river flowing over the edge of a large rock or cliff.

western hemisphere the western half of the earth.

PHOTO CREDITS

t=top; b=bottom; c=centre; l=left; r=right